SUBURBAN 100

SUBURBAN 100

PAUL WELLER

C

CENTURY

LONDON

Published by Century 2007

2 4 6 8 10 9 7 5 3 1

First published in Great Britain in 2007 by Century
Random House, 20 Vauxhall Bridge Road,
London SW1V 2SA

www.rbooks.co.uk

Addresses for companies within The Random House Group Limited
can be found at: www.randomhouse.co.uk/offices.htm

The Random House Group Limited Reg. No. 954009

A CIP catalogue record for this book
is available from the British Library

ISBN 9781846052897

The Random House Group Limited makes every effort to ensure that
the papers used in its books are made from trees that have been legally
sourced from well-managed and credibly certified forests.
Our paper procurement policy can be found at:
www.randomhouse.co.uk/paper.htm

Printed in Italy by L.E.G.O.

WITH THANKS TO HANNAH BLACK, PETER BLAKE, SUZANNE DEAN, JOHN WILSON
AND ALL THOSE WHO HELPED TO PUT THIS BOOK TOGETHER.

Suburban 100

The suburbs – the outskirts, the overspill, the no-man's land of belonging. Sandwiched between neon-lit nights in the big city and the dewy dawns of rural contemplation, suburbia has long struggled to claim art on its side. What can it possibly offer the poetic imagination? How about corner shops and lite-bite cafés, punctured footballs and rusting bicycles, creaking swings and lost laughter on the breeze? All that and more, observed with affection and despair by the finest chronicler of English suburban life that the art of pop music has produced.

Paul Weller made his mark in 1977, declaring that the city was the place to be, a haven for the 'young idea'. But *In The City*, his debut single with The Jam, betrayed the frustrations of a kid wanting to escape the clutches of a small-town upbringing as much as it expressed a metropolitan infatuation. Eighteen-year-old Paul Weller even spelled out his dilemma on the debut album track, *Sounds From The Street*:

I know I come from Woking and you'll say I'm a fraud
But my heart is in the city where it belongs

That lyric is absent from this collection, as is *In The City* itself, *The Modern World* and the 'youth explosion' of *All Around The World*. No doubt he was teenager in genuine thrall to the city; there are stories told of a young Weller walking the capital's streets with a tape recorder to capture the urban clatter and rumble, to be replayed in his bedroom in the family's Surrey council house. And when The Jam rode the first waves of punk rock, Paul moved to London to be at the heart of the action. Yet it was only when he was forced back into suburban exile, stung first by a lacklustre critical response to the band's hastily re-corded second album and then by a withering record company verdict on the next set of demos – 'this is shit' – that he found his true voice as a writer. It wouldn't be the last time Paul Weller had to head back to suburban home turf in search of artistic inspiration.

1978 was the watershed year. Taking stock of life and love, Paul began to write about what he knew, rather than emulate the urban anthems of hate and war and anarchy in the UK. Woking became a canvas on which to paint everyday scenes, to depict lives not so very different from those of his growing audience. It's often said that The Jam were a great singles band, setting ever rising standards at 45rpm. It's true, they were. But they were also a great suburban band which, for five years, set young hearts pumping and inquisitive minds racing in youth clubs and playgrounds. They had the look – sharp, mono-chrome and effortlessly cool; they had the sound – terse, rhythmic and addictively melodic; but above all they had the lyrics.

Paul Weller, who'd left school without a single academic qualifica-tion, emerged from the embers of punk as a pop poet, the creator of extraordinarily deft narratives and bittersweet vignettes. The earliest lyric in this selection is *Down In The Tube Station At Midnight*, a story of fascistic brutality. Told in the first person, from the victim's viewpoint, it recounts a mindless assault on a man on his way home to a suburban home where his wife is 'polishing the cutlery and pulling out the cork'. The verses are tightly structured and the finely observed detail – the toffee wrappers and this morning's papers, the fumble for change, the posters advertising a much-needed getaway – is piled densely in a tor-rent of words that build to an appalling climax. Paul was barely nineteen years old when he wrote *Tube Station*. It was a dramatic curtain-raiser for a writing career that has now continued for three decades.

There are a few figures in the pop world who guard their privacy so fiercely, refuse to pander to expectation and – as Pete Townshend once observed – maintain such a rigid guard against hypocrisy as Paul Weller. There was amazement, tears and rage when, aged twenty-four, he split The Jam at the height of their fame, but the fate of the band had been foretold in their very first single, *In The City*, in which Weller sang that 'all the golden faces are under 25'. He kept to his word.

Young Jam fans who asked their idol about the meaning of his lyrics often had their question returned to them: 'Well, what do you think?' When I was growing up in the suburbs, just beyond north London's outermost fringe, verses were religiously copied out from lyric sheet to school notebook, to be pored over and debated in hunched groups in playground corners. *Thick As Thieves* read like a warning shot, a story of male friendship bound by dreams and unravelled by the harsh realities of adulthood. When, recently, I made a BBC Radio 4 programme about the art and craft of the English pop song, I talked to the poet Simon Armitage and was amazed when he recited the lyrics to *Thick As Thieves* without prompting. Like thousands of other sub-urban boys of the late seventies, he'd recognised himself in Weller's prophetic tale of comradeship crumbling under a 'burning sun in the open sky ... the twinkling stars in the black night'...

But something came along that changed our minds
I don't know what and I don't know why
And we seemed to grow up in a flash of time
As we watched our ideals helplessly unwind

'That's not the sort of lyric you'd normally expect from a pop song, it's way above that, it's a terrific standard of writing', says Simon Armitage. 'I think it was so fantastically judged by Weller. He must have known, even subconsciously, that a lot of people who were listening to The Jam must have been going through that experience, that you have to leave your past behind if you want to learn and develop and grow as a person. Maybe he was also applying that to the country as a whole.'

Alongside the fatalistic resignation and despair that hangs over *Wasteland, Man In The Corner Shop* and *Saturday's Kids*, there is innocence reclaimed and redemption sought in the secret places of Paul Weller's imagination – the 'demi-monde' of *Fly*, the 'pastel fields' of *Tales From The Riverbank*.

Amidst the apocalyptic posturing of his post-punk peers, Weller was an unashamed romantic lyricist, one who wrote of 'feeding ducks in the park and wishing you were far away' in *That's Entertainment*. He's an acute observer and his ability to imagine himself into the lives of others is often astonishing. *Burning Sky* is written as a patronising letter from a businessman too busy climbing the greasy pole to reconnect with old friends:

... and the values that we had once upon a time seem stupid now 'cause the rent must be paid and some bonds severed and others made

Private Hell eavesdrops on the daily routine of a bored housewife, mourning her lost looks and pining for the children who have fled the nest:

The morning slips away in a valium haze
Of catalogues and numerous cups of coffee.
In the afternoon the weekly food
is put in bags
As you float off down the high street
The shop windows reflect, play a nameless host to a closet ghost
A picture of your fantasy

A victim of your misery and
Private hell

A caustic eye is frequently cast over the plight of ordinary people, the ones he sees 'scrimping and saving and crossing off lists'. The observations of injustice took on an increasingly strident political perspective throughout the 1980s, but at their best the lyrics were always imbued with empathy and – influenced by George Orwell, whose idyllic 'golden country' is explored in *Riverbank* – underpinned by the politics of common decency.

For ten consecutive years, from *All Mod Cons* in 1978 until the Style Council's musical adventures, wry humour, costume changes and politics were confusing even the most ardent fan, Paul Weller was a major pop player. As the sales dipped and the backlash whipped in, he headed off to the same place he'd sought solace and inspiration a decade before. 'I took a trip down Boundary Lane, trying to find myself again' were the opening words of the first solo album, reflecting a return to the suburban high streets and bridlepaths, the concrete and conifers that had defined his Woking childhood. *Shadow of the Sun* took the imagery further still, 'chasing dreams across the fields in the shadow of the sun'. And, of course, there's *Stanley Road*, the album which re-established him as a dominant and influential force in British music. On the title track, Paul transports himself back to his own beginnings, to the two-up-two-down terraced house just yards from the mainline tracks that lead to London:

The rolling stock rocked me to sleep
Amber lights flashing across the street
And on the corner a dream to meet
Going on and on

5

This collection of lyrics starts there, with the hazy mist that hangs down the street, shimmering in the sun and suggesting infinite possibilities. We pass through a mystical realm of childhood hopes and dreams, through the suburban roads on which bittersweet domestic dramas are played out. Lovers are embraced, hearts are broken, confidence is rocked, self-doubts are repeatedly interrogated and children are born into a fractured and frightening world.

Paul Weller may be among the most guarded and self effacing of public figures and yet, since 1978, he's consistently revealed himself in song. This collection contains a narrative of sorts. *Suburban 100* is his story. But it's also yours and mine.

John Wilson
June 2007

CONTENTS

CONTENTS

SUBURBAN 100

STANLEY ROAD (1995)

A hazy mist hung down the street
The length of its mile as far as my eye could see
The sky so wide, the houses tall
Or so they seemed to be,
So they seemed to me so small
And it gleamed in the distance and it shone like the sun
Like silver and gold
It went on and on

The summer nights that seemed so long
Always call me back to return as I rewrite this song
The ghosts of night, the dreams of day
Make me swirl and fall and hold me in their sway
And it's still in the distance and it shines like the sun
Like silver and gold
It goes on and on

The rolling stock rocked me to sleep
Amber lights flashing across the street
And on the corner a dream to meet
Going on and on

It goes on and on
on and on
on and on

When I was kid I remember asking my dad how long a mile was. He took me out into our street, Stanley Road in Woking, and pointed down to the far end, towards the heat haze in the far distance. To me there was a magical kingdom through that shimmering haze, the rest of the world, all life's possibilities. I always return to where I came from, to get a sense of my journey and where I'm heading next.

AMONGST BUTTERFLIES (1992)

The sunny sand we ran along
Every day began upon
the summer's kiss of love and adventure
And every dune that we fell into
Left a mark upon us too
Etched forever as a moment we'd remember
And we remember –
The empty woods where we played
Every hour of every day
The holidays went on forever
And in the woods was a soldier's tomb
The ghost of which looked over you
And God was there amongst the trees
We felt his whisper as the summer's breeze
And every night and every day
I learnt to love it in a special way
As I remember what it's like to walk
Amongst butterflies

In the woods, near where we lived, there's a Muslim cemetery for Indian soldiers who served in the First and Second World Wars, slap bang in the middle of the trees. The bodies were removed long ago, because the cemetery was being defaced, but the tomb still stands there as a beautiful ruin. Britain's first mosque was built in Woking, where my mum used to work as a cleaner. This was written as a poem, inspired by memories of a special place.

TALES FROM THE RIVERBANK (1981)

Bring you a tale from the pastel fields
Where we ran when we were young
This is a tale from the water meadows
Spreading love and joy into your heart

It's mixed with happiness, it's mixed with tears
Both life and death are carried in this stream
That open space, you could run for miles
A place of hope in an endless time

The truest of dreams, I live and I wonder
But it's a dream that I always hang on to
That I always run to
Won't you join me by the riverbank

Paradise found down by the still waters
Join in the race to the rainbow's end
No fears to worry in this golden country
Woke at sunrise, went home at sunset

And the magic will weave in
If you start to believe it
The magic between us
The magic of innocence

The truest of dreams, I live and I wonder
But it's a dream that I always hang on to
That I always run to
Won't you join me by the riverbank
Come on and join me by the riverbank

I would have written this is my flat in Pimlico, where I worked on most of the lyrics from the Jam period, thinking back to the rivers and canals around Woking. It's a conscious reference to Kenneth Graham, although I came to him not through school but through Syd Barrett and Pink Floyd, Piper at the Gates of Dawn *...*

PAN (2005)

He is not the God of creation
But he is the Lord of the morning light
And with his song that floats on up
Through the daybreak
It is he that will stay day-long

Through the dawn's early mists
That rise with the river
Through the sound of the world
Once more awake
You can feel his presence strong
As forever, as once more
The ice of night time melts

Give way the day
Give way the day
As we start again

Is he not the God of creation?

... the smell rising from the river, the mist of the evening, the colour of the light coming through the trees in the morning – it's all mystical to me. There's a brilliant passage in The Wind In the Willows *where they've been up all night and, just as the sun's coming up, they meet Pan. They're drawn to him by beautiful, strange music coming through the reeds. It ends with the line 'still, as he looked, he lived; and still, as he lived, he wondered'. I lifted those for another song actually, one on the first solo album. What that phrase really means to me I couldn't tell you, I just know it's about me and how I feel about life. So even though Pan is not the God Almighty, here I've cast him as the God of each new morning and a symbol of rebirth.*

FLY (1978)

The way the sunlight flits across your skirt
Makes me feel I'm from another world
To touch your face in the morning light
I hope you're always gonna be around

The times I struggle to understand why
The ancient proverbs like who am I
Why am I here and what have I done
I see the answers, place my trust in you

Trust in you love
              be with me then
That's when I want you
              that's when I need you the most

I want us to be like Peter Pan
But dreams, it seems, are weightless as sand
And man supposedly is made of sand
It seems that man cannot survive at all

Let's disappear love
              let's fly away
Into the demi-monde
              into the twilight zone

The times inside I spent screaming at you
Release me please from this mortal jail
One shrug or smile can determine my fate
I'm lost for days and have myself to blame

Something I'm giving
     is yours for the taking
Something like sunlight
     love is a spotlight
Love is all sorrow
     still I'll meet you tomorrow
And look forward to see you
     now I can't live without you

At the time, 1978, everything was all fast and furious and we were one of the only bands doing ballads, singing love songs. I was brought up on the Beatles, so I always thought it was OK to mix up an album, to have really hard numbers followed by delicate, tender things.

COUNTRY (1993)

I know a place not far from here
Where life's sweet perfume fills the air
And, if you want, I'll take you there
If you want I'll take you there

Into the light out of the dark
Where only love can heal your heart
And if you want I'll make a start
If you want I'll make a start

This place I say, half hour away
Is that so far to go so near?
And further on we'll find the time
And lose the discontent we feel

I feel the time we've yet to reach
Is not yet within our own belief
But I feel sure that time will come
If it goes on at all

I know a place not far from here
Where fresh cut grass will fill your hair
And if you want we'll lay a while there
    if you want we'll lay a while there

In the early nineties, I started to go back to my home town and revisit many of the places that were special to me as a kid. Just outside Woking there is some of the most beautiful countryside I've ever seen and I've always felt this is the place to recharge and re-align my world vision.

PICKING UP STICKS (2000)

Come blackest crow, start the wheat field to blow
In a wind so high, it waves and glows
'til you can't see the wood for the trees
I'm like anybody on their knees
Trying to find a way to make it fit
    picking up sticks

Let's swirl again, take us far away
To the church bells' chime in a far distant field
To a place where so lately, so slow
And a time I feel like letting it go
Far away enough to catch our breath
I know where and everyone there
Looking to click
    picking up sticks

Come crimson rays, paint us all the same
You know the magic is why and it's here again
Now you can't see the wood for the trees
Now like anybody on their knees
Far away enough to catch our breath
Looking to click
    picking up sticks

Sometimes inspiration comes simply by looking out of a window. This is what I saw where I was living at the time, all the images were there for the taking – the crimson rays, the black crow singing outside my door, the waving wheatfields. It's part Van Gogh, part acid trip.

THICK AS THIEVES (1979)

Times were so tough but not as tough as they are now
We were so close and nothing came between us and the world
No personal situations
Thick as thieves us, we'd stick together for all time
And we meant it but it turns out, just for a while
We stole the friendship that bound us together

We stole from the schools and the libraries
We stole from the drugs that sent us to sleep
We stole from the drink that made us sick
We stole anything that we couldn't keep
And it was enough, we didn't have to spoil anything
And always be as thick as thieves

Like a perfect stranger you came into my life
Then like the perfect lone ranger
You rode away, rode away

We stole the love from young girls in ivory towers
We stole autumn leaves and summer showers
We stole the silent wind that says you are free
We stole everything that we could see
But it wasn't enough and now we've gone and spoiled everything
And we're no longer as thick as thieves

You came into my life
And like a perfect stranger
You walked away, walked away

Thick as thieves us, we'd stick together for all time
And we meant it but it turns out, just for a while
We stole the friendship that bound us together

We stole the burning sun in the open sky
We stole the twinkling stars in the black night
We stole the green-belt fields that made us believe
We stole everything that we could see
But something came along that changed our minds
I don't know what and I don't know why
But we seemed to grow up in a flash of time
As we watched our ideals helplessly unwind

Now we're no longer as thick as thieves
We're not as thick as we used to be
It wasn't enough and we've gone and spoiled everything
Now we're no longer as thick as thieves

Often, when I'm writing, I'm not conscious of what I'm doing after I've started off with the bare bones of an idea. This probably took a few hours of intensive writing, an evening maybe. When I get into that state, it's almost like automatic writing, where I'm connected to something I don't understand, out of my control.

This lyric was central to the concept of Setting Sons, *the lives of three mates who head in different directions. It was inspired by the original group – me, Steve Brookes and Dave Waller – who started The Jam as kids. We set ourselves apart from everyone, we thought we were special, we were going to rule the world. But, of course, people change and friend-ships dissipate.*

WASTELAND (1979)

Meet me on the wasteland later this day
We'll sit and talk and hold hands maybe
For there's not much else to do
in this drab and colourless place
We'll sit amongst the rubber tyres
Amongst the discarded bric-a-brac
people have no use for
Amongst the smouldering embers of yesterday

And when or if the sun shines
Lighting our once beautiful features
We'll smile, but only for seconds
For to be caught smiling is to acknowledge life
A brave but useless show of compassion
And that is forbidden in this drab and colourless world

Meet me on the wastelands, the ones behind
The old houses, the ones left standing pre-war
The ones overshadowed by the monolith monstrosities
councils call homes

And there amongst the shit
the dirty linen
the holy coca-cola tins
the punctured footballs
the ragged dolls
the rusting bicycles
We'll sit and probably hold hands
And watch the rain fall –
tumble and fall
Like our lives –
just like our lives

We'll talk about the old days when the wasteland was release
When we could play and think without feeling guilty
Meet me later, but we'll have to hold hands
And tumble and fall –
Like our lives –
exactly like our lives

I was writing a lot of poetry at this time, set up a publishing company, Riot Stories, and put out a few poetry fanzines. The Liverpool poets were a big influence, Adrian Henri especially. I loved the way they matched the grand ideas with everyday, mundane imagery. Brian Patten wrote a great poem called Somewhere Between Heaven and Woolworth's, *I always got off on that.*

WILD WOOD (1993)

High tide, mid afternoon
People fly by in the traffic's boom
Knowing just where you're blowing
Getting to where you should be going

Don't let them get you down
Making you feel guilty about
Golden rain will bring you riches
All the good things you deserve now

Climbing, forever trying
Find your way out
Of the wild, wild wood
Now there's no justice
There's only yourself that you can trust in

High tide, mid afternoon
People fly by in the traffic's boom
Knowing just where you're blowing
Getting to where you should be going

Day by day your world fades away
Waiting to feel all the dreams that say
Golden rain will bring you riches
All the good things you deserve now

Climbing, forever trying
You're going to find your way out
Of the wild, wild wood

I was trying to write a modern-day folk song, in the true sense of the term. When I play this live I can tell it means a lot to people, they sometimes take the words from me and raise the roof. The wood becomes a metaphor for life in the city, the tides of people, the boom of the traffic.

PRETTY GREEN (1980)

I've got a pocket full of pretty green
I'm gonna put it in the fruit machine
I'm gonna put it in the juke box
It's gonna play all the records in the hit parade

I've got a pocket full of pretty green
I'm gonna give it to the man behind the counter
He's gonna give me food and water
I'm gonna eat that and look for more

This is the pretty green, this is society
You can do nothing unless it's in the pocket

And they didn't teach me that in school
It's something that I learnt on my own
That power is measured by the pound or the fist
It's as clear as this

I've got a pocket full of pretty green

We suddenly found ourselves in America, sometimes two or three times a year, and it was always a culture shock. We were used to British TV gameshows where they'd be lucky to win a matchbox or a kettle. In the States, contestants were going home with submarines and Cadillacs. I remember watching one of the hosts tip out this huge cash prize with the words 'and here's a big barrel of pretty green for you, folks!' That was it. What a title.

MAN IN THE CORNER SHOP (1980)

Puts up the closed sign does the man in the corner shop
Serves his last then he says good bye to him
He knows it is a hard life
But it's nice to be your own boss really

Walks off home does the last customer
He is jealous of the man in the corner shop
He is sick of working at the factory
Says it must be nice to be your own boss really

Sells cigars to the boss from the factory
He is jealous is the man in the corner shop
He is sick of struggling so hard
Says it must be nice to own a factory

Go to church do the people from the area
All shapes and classes sit and pray together
For here they are all one
For God created all men equal

I was always hung up about class, always regarded the class divisions as the real rot in our society, especially growing up in Woking, where affluence and financial struggle were both very apparent. I remember my mum used to have a thing about vicars, she'd always say 'you never see those fuckers round our way'. In the fourth verse, 'go to church do the people from the area', I was trying to make sense of the irony that, in the Bible, the good book, all men are supposedly created equal.

JUST WHO IS THE FIVE O'CLOCK HERO? (1982)

Hello darlin', I'm home again
Covered in shit and aches and pains
Too knackered to think so give me time to come round
Just give me the living room beat to the TV sound

My hard-earned dough goes on bills and the larder
And that Prince Philip tells us we gotta work harder!
It seems a constant struggle just to exist
Scrimping and saving and crossing off lists

From this window I've seen the whole world pass
From dawn to dusk I've heard the last laugh laughed
I've seen enough tears to wash away this street
I've heard wedding bells crime and a funeral march
When as one life finishes another one starts

Alright then, love, so I'll be off now
It's back to the lunchbox and worker-management rows
There's gotta be more to this old life than this
Scrimping and saving and crossing off lists

This comes from seeing me dad come back from the building site, exhausted, always strug-gling for money to make ends meet. At the time, Prince Philip had just told the ordinary man he needed to pull his socks up and make a bit more effort ... but you never did see Phil on the hod, did you?

DOWN IN THE TUBE STATION AT MIDNIGHT (1978)

The distant echo
of faraway voices boarding faraway trains
To take them home to the ones that they love
and who love them forever
Glazed dirty steps repeat my own and reflect my thoughts
Cold and uninviting, partially naked
Except for toffee wrappers and this morning's papers
Mr. Jones got run down
Headlines of death and sorrow, they tell of tomorrow
Madmen on the rampage

And I'm down in the tube station at midnight

I fumble for change, I pull out the Queen, smiling, beguiling
I put in the money, I pull out a plum
Behind me, whispers in the shadows
Gruff blazing voices hating, waiting
'Hey boy' they shout 'have you got any money?'
and I say
'I've a little money and a take away curry
I'm on my way home to my wife
She'll be lining up the cutlery, you know she's expecting me
Polishing the glasses and pulling out the cork'

And I'm down in the tube station at midnight

I first felt a fist and then a kick,
I could now smell their breath
They smelled of pubs and Wormwood Scrubs
and too many right wing meetings
My life swam around me, it took a look and drowned me
in its own existence
The smell of brown leather, it blended in with the weather
It filled my eyes, ears, nose and mouth
It blocked all my senses
I couldn't see, hear, speak any longer

And I'm down in the tube station at midnight

And the last thing that I saw as I lay there on the floor
Was 'Jesus Saves' painted by some atheist nutter
And a British Rail poster read
'Have an awayday, a cheap holiday, do it today!'
I glanced back on my life and thought about my wife
'cause they took the keys and she'll think it's me

And I'm down in the tube station at midnight

This was written as a long poem, in fact there were even more lyrics than this originally. I intended it as a kind of Play For Today *set to music. It was the first song that made people start to take The Jam seriously, and rightly so. I remember thinking that it was taking pop music to a different level, there were no other songs I knew that worked on that level of detail. It's really about my own paranoia about being a suburban kid moving up to the big city, having to watch my arse every time I went out.*

SHOPPING (1982)

High town, high street connections
With clothes at the top of my list
You can steal things from the jewellery department
But you can't take kind or steal a kiss

As I flit from shop window to window
I'm trying to pick up a friendly bargain
But it's not like the adverts all make out
And there's no one to greet you as a friend

I dress myself for the part
I smile but it just don't work
Something about my face must just be the wrong shape
I better try another brand pretty quick

I'm haunted by the colour ad hoardings
A reminder that I must be inadequate
High town, high street connection
With clothes at the top of my list

What a great premise, to write a song called Shopping, *just a celebration of shopping! But I always seemed to have to add a bitter twist in those days, to make it more serious. Now I'd be happy to write a song simply about going shopping.*

FRIDAY STREET (1997)

Minds alive on Friday Street
Summer-flies around my feet
And wee still stars are in my eyes
Minds alive on Friday Street

A pulse goes on in Friday Street
Time seems long against its beat
It's easy to remember
And it's hard to forget
That mine's still alive on Friday Street
Yeah! Mine's still alive on Friday Street

I see myself and it seems so clear
I can walk through the world like I'm not really here
And I really don't care
'cause mine's still alive on Friday Street

Lives alive on Friday Street
You start to shine in a brand new heat
And the world is clear, like you're not really here
And I see myself
And I'm really not scared
'cause mine's still alive on Friday Street
Mine's still alive on Friday Street
It's like plugging back in on Friday Street
May it always come alive on Friday Street

Another one that started from the title. Friday Street is a tiny hamlet in the Surrey country-side, really remote. I was driving through and saw the road-sign and just went, yes! For me, the lyric's about music and playing live, but it's intended to be about whatever you love in life, about reconnecting with a spirit of hope, joy and love.

SATURDAY'S KIDS (1979)

Saturday's boys live life with insults
Drink lots of beer and wait for half-time results
Afternoon tea in the light-a-bite –
chat up the girls –
They dig it!

Saturday's girls work in Tesco's and Woolworth's
Wear cheap perfume 'cause it's all they can afford
Go to discos, they drink Babycham –
talk to Jan –
In bingo accents!

Saturday's kids play on one-arm-bandits
They never win but that's not the point is it?
Dip in silver paper when their pints go flat –
how about that? –
Far out!

Their mums and dads smoke Capstan non-filters
Wallpaper lives 'cause they all die of cancer
What goes on, what goes wrong?

Save up their money for a holiday
To Selsey Bill or Bracklesham Bay
Think about the future when they'll settle down
Marry the girl next door with one on the way

These are the real creatures
that time has forgot
Not given a thought –
it's the system
hate the system
what's the system?

Saturday's kids live in council houses
Wear v-necked shirts and baggy trousers
Drive Cortinas, fur trimmed dash boards
Stains on the seats
In the back of course!

A lot of the kids I went to school with were simply out for a good time, they didn't give a fuck. But I could see a lot of the boys were heading for dead-end jobs and the girls would be pushing prams at sixteen. I wasn't looking down on them and, in a way, it's a celebration of their lives, but I always knew it wasn't enough for me. I wrote this in Selsey in a caravan, one of my first holidays. I thought that's what you did, I didn't realise you could get on a plane and go somewhere nice, I thought planes were just for touring with the band. Of course it rained all week, so I sat in the caravan and came away with three or four songs. Eton Rifles was written during the same holiday.

BACK IN THE FIRE (2000)

Dreams, schemes and everythings
Fill the dusty corners of your mind
As cars, boats and aeroplanes
Just remind you of a better time
As loves, hopes and everyone
Anyone worth a minute of your time
When unhampered by the agents
Of the governors, of the faceless, so opaque
As bare trees and winter winds
Just confine you to a bitter place
A time you can't face
No peace in your mind

We should be playing in the sunshine
Happy to be part of everything
Not handled – greedy handlers –
Brought down and destroyed by their own ways
Liars! Liars! Smoking on pipes
Dimmed fires who just throw it all their way
And how's your father today
Was he caught in the rain
Waiting on a bed, putting up with the pain
Your three wishes expired
Now you're back in the fire
Locked the genie in the shed
Put a pistol to his head

Not handcuffed to some wanker
Who doesn't know me and doesn't see our lives are made
On all the efforts of the masses
And all the people who deserve a better fate
Than a time you can't trace
No peace in your mind
A time you can't place
Now you're back in the race
Your three wishes expired
Now you're back in the fire
Your three wishes expired
Now you're back in the fire

See, you just can't play now without a say
Always got to be the man
Always got to have the plan
It doesn't run that way
Into the ether you'll stay
Your three wishes expired
Now you're back in the fire

People are still chewed up and spat out after working all their lives, paying their taxes, helping their community and country, only to be left waiting in grotty hospital corridors, literally dying for a bed. The idea of the genie in the shed, it's back to the Liverpool poets again, to 'Heaven and Woolworth's'.

THE PLANNER'S DREAM GOES WRONG (1982)

Letting loose the lunatics wasn't the greatest of ideas
Giving them plans and money to squander
Should have been the worst of our fears –
The dream life, luxury living
Was a pleasant No.10 whim
But somewhere down the line of production
They left out human beings

They were gonna build communities
It was going to be pie in the sky
But the piss-stench hallways and broken-down lifts
Say the planner's dream went wrong

If people were meant to live in boxes
God would have given them string
To tie around themselves at bed time
And stop their dreams falling through the ceiling

And the public schoolboy computers
Keep spewing out our future
The house in the country designs the 14th floor
Old Mrs. Smith don't get out much more
Coitus interruptus 'cause of next door's rows
Your washing gets nicked when the lights go out
Babies scream in the nightmare throng
But the planners just get embarrassed
         when their plans go wrong

Luckily for them, the people who design the scary concrete jungles can all go back to their mock-Tudor country homes at the weekend.

SET THE HOUSE ABLAZE (1980)

I was in the pub last night
A mutual friend of ours said
he'd seen you in the uniform
Yeah, the leather belt looks manly
The black boots butch
But, oh what a bastard to get off
Promises, promises, they offer real solutions
But hatred has never won for long

You were so open-minded
But by someone, blinded
And now your sign says closed
Promises, promises, they offer real solutions
But hatred has never won for long

I think we've lost our perception
I think we've lost sight of the goals we should be working for
I think we've lost our reason
We stumble blindly and vision must be restored

I wish that there was something I could do about it
I wish that there was some way I could try to fight it
scream and shout it –
But something you said set the house ablaze!

This was about the rise of the neo-Nazi groups of the late 70s, early 80s. I'd talk to some kids at gigs who you could tell had just been indoctrinated and had their anger and frustrations fuelled by cynical maniacs. It was pretty fucking scary and still is. I tried to work in a bit of William Blake in the second half – a true visionary.

HERE'S ONE THAT GOT AWAY (1984)

The pub talk, the scandals
Like vandals they try to tear you down
The whispers turn rumours
There's no truth but that don't stop those cats
They need that little bit extra
They don't mind if it's only conjecture

They tried to tell me I wasn't full-time
I tried to think of an alibi
I felt so awful I spat in their faces and ran for my life

They tried to tell me theirs was the right way
I tried to shout that was a lie
I felt so sick I spat on their lifestyles with a runaway pride!

Untouched by human hands
'cause only God knows I don't call that a man
Who spends his waking days
Telling others what to think and what to say

They tried to tell me I wasn't normal
I tried to shout there's no such thing!
I felt so sick I spat on their lifestyles with a runaway pride
So catch me if you can
'cause I would rather be dead than live like that

It's like Saturday's Kids, *the idea that I may not have been born into privilege and education but I was going to break away from what I had been offered. Music was my route out.*

WHEN YOU'RE YOUNG (1979)

Life is timeless, days are long when you're young
You used to fall in love with everyone
Any guitar and any bass drum
Life is a drink and you get drunk
when you're young

Life is new and there's things to be done
You can't wait to be grown up
Acceptance into the capital world
You pull on some weed then you pull on someone
when you're young

But you find out life isn't like that, it's so hard to comprehend
Why you set up your dreams to have them smashed in the end
But you don't mind, you've got time on your side
And they're never gonna make you stand in line
You're just waiting for the right time

You're fearless and brave, you can't be stopped when you're young
You swear you're never ever gonna work for someone
No corporations for the new age sons
Tears of rage roll down your face but
still you say it's fun

And you find out life isn't like that, it's so hard to understand
Why the world is your oyster but your future's a clam
It's got you in its grip before you're born
It's done with the use of a dice and a board
They let you think you're king but you're really a pawn

You're fearless and brave, you can't be stopped when you're young
You used to fall in love with everyone
Any guitar and any bass drum

There were certain times during the The Jam, which was an intense, pressurised period, when we just needed a single and I had to write to order. Sometimes, when your back's against the wall, you surprise yourself. I'm ambivalent about this one now though. It's about growing up and I suppose I was just going through the same things as the people listening to it – the tears of rage – which may be why a lot of people connected to this lyric.

TO BE SOMEONE (1978)

To be someone must be a wonderful thing
A famous footballer, a rock singer or a big film star
Yes I think I would like that!

To be rich and have lots of fans
Have lots of girls to prove that I'm a man
And be number one and liked by everyone

Getting drugged up with my trendy friends
They really dig me man and I dig them
And the bread I spend is like my fame –
It's quickly diminished

There's no more swimming in a guitar-shaped pool
No more reporters at my beck and call
No more cocaine, now it's only ground chalk
No more taxis, now we'll have to walk

But didn't we have a nice time
Didn't we have a nice time
Oh, wasn't it such a fine time

I realise I should have stuck to my guns
Instead shit out to be one of the bastard sons
And lose myself, I know it was wrong –
But it's cost me a lot

There's no more drinking when the club shuts down
I'm out on my arse with the rest of the clowns
It's really frightening without a bodyguard
So I stay confined to my lonely room

To be someone must be a wonderful thing

*This wasn't about me, The Jam were only just on the cusp of stardom at the time. This was
me being cynical, guarding myself against becoming like this, a warning to myself. But it's
also written from a standpoint of naivety. At the time, I was trying to project myself into
other characters, as Ray Davies had done. I was too young to be writing about myself.*

HE'S THE KEEPER (2000)

He's the keeper of the lantern
Stone believer, it's a passion
And he knows it, he's the keeper
Hanging wishes upon our stars
As he waits for love
    yes he waits for love

Flying without a hand
Trying to brave the land
Something about the man
Is about to make a stand!
With nothing but liars and thieves
Trying to purchase thee
Where are you meant to go
But fly away, high away

He's the one knight on a knackered stallion
His rusty armour so undervalued
Does he know that he's a reason
He's asleep now but never gone
He just waits for love,
    yes he waits for love

Hanging without a cloud
Hoping to draw a crowd
If he's willing to take a chance
– come on people make a stance!

From tiny acorns grow
All kinds of seekers
And where are they meant go
But fly away, high away

In the maelstrom of indecision
Shine, believer! Find the season
He helped to grow it, he's the keeper
Hanging wishes up upon our stars
As he waits for love,
    yes we wait for love

He's the keeper of the lantern
He's the message in the midnight
of your madness
In the backlog of conversations
we never had
We wait for love,
    yes we wait for love

I wrote this about Ronnie Lane after I'd heard of his passing. I love all the Small Faces, but there is an air of the romantic and the spiritual in Ronnie's songs and life which I find beautiful and inspiring. That, regardless of where you are born and how you speak, you can still be a seeker in life and it's not just the property of the intellectual and educated classes. In the lyrics there are also references to his Passing Show, *his spiritual journey and, in the second verse, a reference to* Don Quixote, *which I think he would have liked. I hope so, God bless him.*

A MAN OF GREAT PROMISE (1985)

I bought the paper yesterday
and I saw the obituary
And I read of how you died in pain
Well, I just couldn't understand it

If I could have changed that
Then Lord knows I'd do it now
But there is no going back
And what's done is done forever

You were always chained and shackled by the dirt
Of every small-town institution and every big-town flirt

And I think of what you might have been –
a man of such great promise
Oh, but you seemed to forget the dream
And the more you saw, you hated
But let's not talk of blame for what is only natural
Like a moth going to a flame
You had a dangerous passion

You were always chained and shackled by the dirt
Of every small-town institution and every big-town flirt

All the things that you might have been
But who am I to say?
– still I wonder –
If it's in the cold earth you prefer to lay
If it's in the cold earth you prefer to stay

Dave Waller was in The Jam in the early days and this is a song which mourns his passing.
He was a poet, a very talented one, but heroin put a stop to all he had.

BURNING SKY (1979)

Dear –

How are things in your little world, I hope they're going well and you are too. Do you still see the same old crowd, the ones who used to meet every Friday, I'm really sorry that I can't be there but work comes first, I'm sure you'll understand. Things are really taking off for me, business is thriving and I'm showing a profit and in any case it wouldn't be the same, 'cause we've all grown up and we've got our own lives and the values that we had once upon a time seem stupid now 'cause the rent must be paid and some bonds severed and others made.

Now, I don't want you to get me wrong, ideals are fine when you are young, though I must admit that we had a laugh but that's all it was and ever will be, 'cause the burning sky keeps burning bright and as long as it does (and it always will) there's no time for dreams when commerce calls and the taxman's shouting 'cause he wants his dough and the wheels of finance won't begin to slow. And it's only us realists who are gonna come through 'cause there's only one power higher than that of truth and that's the burning sky.

Oh, by the way I must tell you before I sign off that I've got a meeting next week with the head of a big corporate, I can't disclose who but I'm sure you'll know it. And the burning sky keeps burning bright and it won't turn off 'til it's had enough, it's the greedy bastard that won't give up and you're just a dreamer if you don't realise and the sooner you do will be the better for you; then we'll all be happy and we'll all be wise and we'll all bow down to the burning sky.

Then we'll all be happy and we'll all be wise and together we will live beneath the burning sky.

Yours –

This was another key lyric in the Setting Sons *concept of the three friends who split up and go their separate ways. This is the successful one, who makes his mark in business. I wrote it as a letter and I hadn't seen that done before, so the music had to fit the unconventional structure. It was ambitious. Setting Sons – the literary years!*

THE ETON RIFLES (1979)

Sup up your beer and collect your fags
There's a row going on down near Slough
Get out your mat and pray to the West
I'll get out mine and pray for myself

Thought you were smart when you took them on
But you didn't take a peep in their artillery room
All that rugby puts hairs on your chest
What chance have you got against a tie and a crest?

Hello, hooray, what a nice day
For the Eton Rifles
Hello, hooray, I hope rain stops play
For the Eton Rifles

Thought you were clever when you lit the fuse
Tore down the House of Commons in your brand new shoes
Composed a revolutionary symphony
Then went to bed with a charming young thing

Hello, hooray, cheers then mate
It's the Eton Rifles
Hello, hooray, an extremist scrape
With the Eton Rifles

What a catalyst you turned out to be
Loaded the guns then you ran off home for your tea
Left me standing like a guilty schoolboy

We came out of it naturally the worst
Beaten and bloody and I was sick down my shirt
We were no match for their untamed wit
Though some of the lads said they'd be back next week

Hello, hooray, there's a price to pay
To the Eton Rifles
Hello hooray I'd prefer the plague
To the Eton Rifles

The caravan years! Written in Selsey, like Saturday's Kids. *The story was there for me already – the unemployment march started out in Liverpool and passed Eton college. All the young chaps came out to jeer and take the piss. It was a mini class war being played out. It's supposed to be a funny song, but there's also real sense of resignation to it – what chance have you got against a tie and a crest? – the establishment will always win. I wrote it in one go as it reads on the page, starting with that opening couplet.*

THE BUTTERFLY COLLECTOR (1979)

So you've finally got what you wanted
You've achieved your aim by making the walking lame
And when you just can't get any higher
You use your senses to suss out this week's climber
And the small fame that you've acquired
Has brought you into cult status
But to me you're still a collector

There's tarts and whores but you're much more
You're a different kind 'cause you want their minds
And you just don't care 'cause you've got no pride
It's just a face on your pillowcase
that thrills you

And you started looking much older
And your fashion sense is second-rate like your perfume
But to you in your own little dream world
You're still the queen of the butterfly collectors

As you carry on 'cause its all you know
You can't light a fire, you can't cook or sew
You get from day to day by filling your head
But surely you must know the appeal between your legs
has worn off

And I don't care about morals
'cause the world's insane and we're all to blame anyway
And I don't feel any sorrow
Towards the kings and queens of the butterfly collectors

This is about a groupie girl from the punk days. Looking back on it now, it's a bit harsh, because she was actually really nice! But I just took her and exaggerated.

LIZA RADLEY (1980)

Liza Radley, see the girl with long hair
See her creeping 'cross summer lawns at midnight
And all the people in the town where we live say
She's not quite right, she don't fit in with a small town
They just can't understand why she doesn't say much
But in a darkened room it's for their lives only
she cries

Liza Radley, see her jump through loneliness
Liza Radley, take me when you go
And as the people pass by, their heads in the air
Haunted with their noise, she recalls a lonely sigh
But no matter what they say
In her mind she knows their dream of life
They won't ever find

Liza Radley, I pledge myself to you alone
She kissed my face and said love means nothing at all
She kissed my face and said life means nothing at all

A totally imaginary character, a special person caught up in the small town clutches. She's haunted by the lives around her and disturbed that they're wasting themselves.

GIRL ON THE PHONE (1979)

Girl on the phone keeps a'ringing back
Her voice is smooth but the tone is flat
She's telling me this and she's telling me that
She talks about me and I must agree
With what she says about me
About how nice I can be
But it makes no difference
to my mind

Girl on the phone keeps a'ringing back
She knows all my details, she's got my facts
She tells me my height and she knows my weight
She knows my age and says she knows my fate
And I must say its logical
What foresight she must have
I've got to meet her whenever
I get time

Says she knows everything about me
Every word I've ever said
Every book I've ever read
She told me that we met a long time ago
I can't think when but she should know

Girl on the phone keeps a'ringing back
Knows where I get my shirts and where I get my pants
Where I get my trousers where I get socks
My leg measurement and the size of my cock

And I must say it's unnerving
To think that she knows me
Knows me so well, better than anyone
Better than myself

Girl on the phone keeps a'ringing back
She's telling me this and she's telling me that

We were making Setting Sons *and needed two more songs for the album. I remember going into an empty office at our old management place which had just a desk and a chair. I sat down and wrote this and* Private Hell *in one go. This one was a bit of comic light relief from the rest of the album, which was all very serious. I didn't intend it to be about a stalker and I certainly didn't have anyone calling me up at night. It all came from the title, which was lifted from the Roy Lichtenstein painting of the girl on the phone.*

A WOMAN'S SONG (1987)

Hush little baby, don't you cry
Momma's gonna buy you a nursery rhyme
And if that don't send you to sleep
Momma's gonna have to find the keep.
All of our worries are not our choice
Someone sees to that, I know not why
Things that we worked for, they've started to sell
Now heaven is for angels and earth is hell.
Hush little baby, your time may come
When things, as they are now, will be undone
And you as the change if you last that long
    you as the change if you last that long.
Hush oh my child, momma's only sad
They've damned nearly taken away all I had
and all I have in the world is you
It's you and the future that sees me through
All I have in the world is you
It's you and the future that sees me through

*It my update of the nursery rhyme, hush little baby don't you cry. A single mum struggling
and kept going only by the love of her child.*

PRIVATE HELL (1979)

Closer than close, you see yourself
A mirrored image of what you wanted to be
As each day goes by, a little more
You can't remember what it was you wanted anyway.
The fingers feel the lines, they prod the space, your ageing face
The face that once was so beautiful
Is still there but unrecognisable
Private hell

The man who you once loved is bald and fat
And seldom in, working late as usual
Your interest has waned, you feel the strain
The bed springs snap
On the occasions he lies upon you
Close your eyes and think of nothing but
Private hell

Think of Emma, wonder what she's doing
Her husband Terry and your grandchildren,
Think of Edward who's still at college
You send him letters which he doesn't acknowledge
'cause he don't care, they don't care
They're all going through their own
Private hell

The morning slips away in a valium haze
Of catalogues and numerous cups of coffee
In the afternoon the weekly food
Is put in bags as you float off down the high street
The shop windows reflect, play a nameless host to a closet ghost
A picture of your fantasy
A victim of your misery and
Private hell

Alone at 6 o'clock
you drop a cup
you see it smash
inside you crack
you can't go on
but you sweep it up

Safe at last inside your
Private hell
Sanity at last inside your
Private hell

This came from a friend of mine whose mother was a small, frail looking lady with an air of the downtrodden. I can't ever remember seeing her smile. The rest of the story is pure imagination, but I suppose I was thinking of a very middle-class dysfunctional family, with parents and children removed and alienated from each other. A house with no love.

THAT'S ENTERTAINMENT (1980)

A police car and a screaming siren
A pneumatic drill and ripped up concrete
A baby wailing and a stray dog howling
The screech of brakes and lamp lights blinking –
that's entertainment

A smash of glass and the rumble of boots
An electric train and a ripped up phone booth
Paint splattered walls and the cry of a tomcat
Lights going out and a kick in the balls –
that's entertainment

Days of speed and slow time Mondays
Pissing down with rain on a boring Wednesday
Watching the news and not eating your tea
A freezing cold flat and damp on the walls –
that's entertainment

Waking up at 6 am on a cool warm morning
Opening the windows and breathing in petrol
An amateur band rehearsing in a nearby yard
Watching the telly and thinking about your holidays –
that's entertainment

Waking up from bad dreams and smoking cigarettes
Cuddling a warm girl and smelling stale perfume
A hot summer's day and sticky black tarmac
Feeding ducks in the park and wishing you were far away –
that's entertainment

Two lovers kissing amongst the scream of midnight
Two lovers missing the tranquility of solitude
Getting a cab and travelling on buses
Reading the graffiti about slashed seat affairs –
that's entertainment

The idea of taking the old Hollywood song and turning it into an urban, mundane tale instead came from a poem by Paul Drew which I published in a fanzine I put out in the early '80s. The images I drew were all directly around me. It didn't take long to write, maybe fifteen, twenty minutes. The words all all came out in one go, but it seems to endure. I think it's the everyday images that people relate to.

A TOWN CALLED MALICE (1981)

You'd better stop dreaming of the quiet life
'cause it's the one we'll never know
And quit running for that runaway bus
Those rosy days are few
And stop apologising for the things you've never done
'cause time is short and life is cruel
But it's up to us to change
This town called malice

Rows and rows of disused milk floats
Stand dying in the dairy yard
And a hundred lonely housewives
Clutch empty milk bottles to their hearts
Hanging out their old love letters on the line to dry
It's enough to make you stop believing
When tears come fast and furious
In a town called malice

Struggle after struggle, year after year
The atmosphere's a fine blend of ice
I'm almost stone cold dead
In a town called malice

A whole street's belief in Sunday's roast beef
Gets dashed against the Co-op
To either cut down on beer or the kids' new gear
It's a big decision
In a town called malice

The ghost of a steam train echoes down my track
It's at the moment bound for nowhere,
Just going round and round
Playground kids and creaking swings
Lost laughter in the breeze
I could go on for hours and I probably will
But I'd sooner put some joy back
In this town called malice

I was trying to capture a sense of the anger that I felt – that a lot of people felt – about Thatcherism and the way that she and the Tory Party at that time were trying to dismantle the communities of the working classes. Attacks on the the trade unions, small businesses disappearing and so many aspects of English life being closed down to people – I was trying to reflect the frustration and despair that sprang out of all that. There was a phoney pretence that we could suddenly all be middle class because we were allowed to buy our own houses, get a mortgage and be in debt for the rest of our lives. I like the suburban images in A Town Called Malice, the rows and rows of disused milk floats, the Co-op. Whether they are absolutely true doesn't matter, they stand as metaphors for what I saw going on.

ALL GONE AWAY (1985)

The wind blows whispers down the street
Having free reign with the town so bleak
Like everything else it's
        all gone away

The town hall clock gives forth it's chime
For no one there to ask the time
Like everything else they've
        all gone away

The grocer's shop hangs up its sign
The sign says closed, it's a sign of the times
Like everything else it's
        all gone away

But somewhere the party never ends
And greedy hands rub together again
Shipping out the profits that they've stolen
An eerie wail comes from the pit
The ghosts of the men who take the morning shift
Just like clockwork, rusting away

Come take a walk upon these hills
And see how monetarism kills
        whole communities
        even families
There's nothing left so they've
        all gone away

If you travelled up North in the mid-80s you could see how hard the Thatcher Gang's economics had hit it. By the end of her tenure, there weren't any vital industries left in this country. It's the roots of why we produce fuck all anymore. And all this was done whilst still flying the flag. Incredibly, she got away with it for eighteen years. I hope she rots in her own hell.

DREAMTIME (1980)

Streets I ran, this whole town
Backstreets and all, I wanted to leave there
But no matter how fast I ran
My feet were glued, I just couldn't move there
I saw the hate and lots of people
I heard my name called above the noise
I tried to speak but my tongue was tied
Bumped into emptiness and started to cry, oh no!

I saw the lights and the pretty girls
And I thought to myself what a pretty world
But there's something else here that puts me off
And I'm so scared dear
My love comes in frozen packs
Bought in a supermarket

Streets I ran, through wind and rain
Around this place amongst steaming sunshine
Scared I was, sweating now
Feeling of doom and my bowels turned to water –
I felt hot breath whisper in my ear
I looked for somewhere to hide but everywhere's closed
I shut my eyes pretend not to be here but
This feeling's much to real to ever disappear, oh no!

Boy, it's a tough, tough world
But you've got to be tough with it

I saw the lights and the pretty girls
And I thought to myself what a pretty world
But there's something else here that puts me off
And I'm so scared dear
My love comes in frozen packs

As a friend once said ... 'enjoy your paranoia'. And in this lyric I did.

THE DREAMS OF CHILDREN (1980)

I sat alone with the dreams of children
Weeping willows and tall dark buildings and
I caught a vision from the dreams of children
But woke up sweating to this modern nightmare and
I was alone, no one was there

I caught a glimpse from the dreams of children
I got a feeling of optimism
But woke up to a grey and lonely picture
The streets below left me feeling dirty and
I was alone, no one was there

Something's gonna crack up your dreams tonight
You will crack on your dreams tonight

I fell in love with the dreams of children
I saw a vision of only happiness
I've caught a fashion from the dreams of children
But woke up sweating from this modern nightmare and
I was alone, no one was there

Something's gonna crack in your dreams tonight
You will crack on your dreams tonight

Writing is also a way of projecting myself into what I would aspire to be, whether spiritually or just as a better person, more caring; able to articulate what I really want to say to people. I don't have those day-to-day skills. I was going through my William Blake / Arthurian phase at the time I wrote this.

FUNERAL PYRE (1981)

Down in amongst the streets tonight
Books will burn, people laugh and cry
In their turmoil
(turmoil turns rejoiceful)
Shed your fears and lose your guilt
Tonight we burn responsibility in the fire
We'll watch the flames grow higher!
But if you get too burnt you can't come back home

And as I was standing by the edge
I could see the faces of those who led
Pissing themselves laughing
Their mad eyes bulged, their flushed faces said
The weak get crushed as the strong grow stronger

We feast on flesh and drink on blood
Live by fear and despise love in a crisis
(what with today's high prices)
Bring some paper and bring some wood
Bring what's left of all your love for the fire
We'll watch the flames grow higher!
But if you get too burnt you can't come back home

And as I was standing by the edge
I could see the faces of those who led
Pissing themselves laughing
Their mad eyes bulged their flushed faces said
The weak get crushed as the strong grow stronger

PAUL WELLER

In the funeral pyre
We'll watch the flames grow higher
But if you get too burnt you can't come back home
In the funeral pyre

I had these images of the Nazi book burnings mixed up with the NF propaganda of the time.

SAVAGES (2005)

Savages, He knows you are
Do you not think that God is looking down
On you savages
As children run to mothers
You put bullets in their backs
Cowards, can you not see
Can you not see that love is coming down?

You have no gods, they've all disowned you
You have no love, so you take it out on
people's lives and progress
That's what keeps you going
When you're savages

Savages, you can dress it up
Give it a name and a fancy uniform
And a flag to fly, to hide behind
Can you not see the truth that's on the ground?

You have no love, it has all gone cold on you
You never had, so you take it out on
Those whose love is growing
And that's what you hate most
When you're savages

Do you not see that love is coming down?

LITTLE BOY SOLDIERS (1979)

It's funny how you never knew what my name was
Our only contact was a form for the election –
These days I find that I don't listen
These days I find that we're out of touch
These days I find that I'm too busy
So why the attention now you want my assistance
– what have you done for me?

You've gone and got yourself in trouble
Now you want me to help you out
These days I find that I can't be bothered
These days I find that it's all too much
To pick up a gun and shoot a stranger
But I've got no choice so here I come
– war games

I'm up on the hills playing little boy soldiers
Reconnaissance duty up at 5.30
Shoot, shoot, shoot and kill the natives
You're one of us and we love you for that
Think of honour, Queen and country
You're a blessed son of the British Empire
God's on our side and so is Washington
Come out on the hills with the little boy soldiers

Come on outside, I'll sing you a lullaby
Or tell a tale of how goodness prevailed
We ruled the world, we killed and robbed
The fucking lot, but we don't feel bad
It was done beneath the flag of democracy
You'll believe and I do, yes I do, yes I do

These days I find that I can't be bothered
To argue with them, well what's the point?
Better to take your shots and drop down dead
Then they'll send you home in a pine overcoat
With a letter to your mum saying find enclosed:
One son, one medal
And a note to say
He won

We played in Germany in '79 while the British forces were still based there. I talked to some young squaddie lads at a soundcheck who told me they thought the words were spot-on. That was good enough for me. They told me they'd all joined because there was no other work where they were from.

WHIRLPOOL'S END (1995)

The sun came out and hung above
Over our heads but far enough to see
A bomb exploding in another town
Children choking on a poison cloud
While on the streets, where lovers once walked
Side by side in idle talk
Bullets fall like unholy rain
People change as the panic sets in
A frightened baby by her dead mother's side
In a brutal world where there's nowhere
To run, hide or cry

Now nothing feels the same way
Feel like I'm changing again
Upon a street with no name
It's hard to find me again

I ran as fast as my feet could fly
Down country lanes where I took my time
Time like a hound snapping at my heels
I got past thinking so that I could feel
And like a film playing in my head
I kept on rolling down green Surrey hills
                              in Spring

Now I don't feel the same way
Feel like I'm changing again
Upon a street with no name
It's hard to find me again

The sun came out and hung above
Over our heads but far enough to see

The sun shines in a lot of my words. I think it's my metaphor for God. 'I got past thinking so that I could feel' was really where I was at this time.

GHOSTS OF DACHAU (1984)

I close my eyes
I reach out my hand
and there you are
beautiful in scabs
caressing my scalp
under the mounts of the gun towers
I shout your name
I kick out in dreams
and here we are –
the searchlight beams
the siren squeals
and a hopeless shuffle to certainty
the crab lice bite
the typhoid smells
and I'm still here
handsome in rags
a trouserless man
waiting helpless for dignity
come to me angel, don't go to the showers
beg, steal or borrow
now there's nothing left to take
except eternity
and who will come
to flower our graves?
with us still here
covered with dust
remembered by few
but forgotten by the majority

stay with me angel
don't get lost in history
don't let all we suffered lose its meaning in the dark
that we call memory

I got the idea for this from a brilliant book called This Way For The Gas, Ladies and Gentlemen *by a Polish writer called Tadeusz Borowski. Even amongst the crime and degradation, there were still love affairs and relationships. I visited Dachau in 1978.*

MONEY-GO-ROUND (1983)

It's no good praying to the powers that be
'cause they won't shake the roots of the money tree
It's no good praying to the pristine altars
Waiting for the blessing with the holy water
The same old wealth in the same old hands
Means the same old people stay in command

Watch the money-go-round, watch the money-go-round
They got it wrapped up tight, they got it safe and sound
Watch the money-go-round, watch the money-go-round
As you fall from grace and hit the ground

Too much money in too few places
Only puts a smile on particular faces
Too much power in not enough hands
Makes me think: get rich quick, take all I can
They're too busy spending on the means of destruction
To ever spend a penny on some real construction

Watch the money-go-round, watch the money-go-round
They amuse themselves as they fool around
Watch the money-go-round, watch the money-go-round
Do like they say, make you vulnerable

No good looking to the Empire corners
Civilisation built on slaughter
Carrying hopes and carrying maps
The spineless ones fall in their laps
The brave and the bold are the ones to be fooled
With a diet of lies from the Kipling school

Watch the money-go-round, watch the money-go-round
But I just can't help being cynical
Watch the money-go-round, watch the money-go-round
Do like I say, make it wonderful

Their morals are clean and their morals clear
They bend your arm and they bend your ear
They bend your mind as they talk in circles
Bend over forwards, this won't hurt you
'til there's blood in your lap, blood on your hands
Their smile says they're done and took all they can

Watch the money-go-round, watch the money-go-round
Come spend a penny, go out with a pound
Watch the money-go-round, watch the money-go-round
As you fall from grace and hit the ground

They need your votes and you know where to send 'em
But we don't get the choice of a public referendum
On all the real issues that affect our lives
Like the USA bases to which we play midwife
Take a Cruise and forget this scene
Come back later when the slate's wiped clean

Watch the money-go-round, watch the money-go-round
Born of woman, killed by man
Watch the money-go-round, watch the money-go-round
Do like they pray, make it wonderful

The good and the righteous sing their hymns
The crimpolene dresses who have no sins
Christians by day, killers in war
The hypocrites who know what they're fighting for
Killing for peace, freedom and truth
But they're too old to go so they send the youth

Watch the money-go-round, watch the money-go-round
I don't think He was an astronaut
Watch the money-go-round, watch the money-go-round
I must insist he was a socialist!

Watch the money-go-round, watch the money-go-round
They got it wrapped up tight, they got it safe and sound
Watch the money-go-round, watch the money-go-round
As you fall from grace and hit the ground

I went through something of a political awakening, a realisation of how the system worked.
I had a lot to say at the time, even if some of it seems a bit naïve reading it now.

GOING UNDERGROUND (1980)

Some people might say my life is in a rut
But I'm quite happy with what I've got
People might say that I should strive for more
But I'm so happy, I can't see the point –
Something's happening here today
A show of strength with your boys' brigade
And I'm so happy and you're so kind
You want more money, of course I don't mind
To buy nuclear textbooks for atomic crimes
And the public gets what the public wants
But I want nothing this society's got –

I'm going underground
Well, let the brass bands play and feet start to pound
I'm going underground
Let the boys all sing, let the boys all shout for tomorrow

Some people might get some pleasure out of hate
Me, I've enough already on my plate
People might need some tension to relax
Me, I'm too busy dodging between the flak
What you see is what you get
You've made your bed, you better lie in it
You choose your leaders and place your trust
As their lies wash you down and their promises rust
You'll see kidney machines replaced by rockets and guns
And the public wants what the public gets
But I don't get what this society wants

I'm going underground
Well the brass bands play and feet start to pound
Going underground
So let the boys all sing and let the boys all shout for tomorrow

We talk and we talk 'til my head explodes
I turn on the news and my body froze
The braying sheep on my TV screen
Make this boy shout, make this boy scream!
I'm going underground

What strikes me is how little has changed. This was a response to Thatcher and Reagan linking arms, the planting of nuclear bases on British soil, all the banging of chests, false nationalism and phoney patriotism.

START! (1980)

It's not important for you to know my name
Nor I to know yours
If we communicate for two minutes only
It will be enough
For knowing that someone in this world
Feels as desperate as me
– and what you give is what you get

It doesn't matter if we never meet again
What we have said will always remain
If we get through for two minutes only
It will be a start!
For knowing that someone in this life
Loves with a passion called hate
– and what you give is what you get

If I never ever see you
If I never ever see you
If I never ever see you again
– and what you give is what you get

I was thinking about the power of music and the power of a pop song, how two or three minutes could say so much to so many. And what it's always meant to me. I was stripping words back to the bare minimum at the time, just getting to the point. Pop music, for want of a better term, is the only art form that can communicate directly and emotionally on that level.

HOMEBREAKERS (1985)

Good morning day, how do you do
I wonder what will you do for me?
I should be on my way, I should be earning pay
I should be all the things that I'm not
And I've tried on my own now there's nothing to keep me at home
Like my brother has too, got to leave to get out of this view
You see, they tell you to move around
If you can't find work in your own town

As I rise from my bed I can hear the old man
Blaming heaven and mother for this
Thirty years with one firm, thirteen months redundant
Yes, I'd say that's unlucky for some

Now our tears fall like rain as my mother walks me to my train
With a kiss and a wave
I'll come home weekends, that's if I can save
I swear I'll take it out on the man
Who ever devised this economy plan.

All the love in the world
Can't put dinner on the table
All the hate that I feel, no love could put right

Good morning day and how do you do
I wonder what will you do for me?
I should be on my way, I should be earning pay
I should be all the things that I'm not
And I've tried on my own, now there's nothing to keep me at home
All the love and the strength has been taken by this government
You see, they tell you to move around
If you can't find work in your own town

Father's in the kitchen, counting out coins
Mother's in the bedroom, looking through pictures of her boys
One is in London, looking for a job
The other's in Whitehall looking for those responsible

This – and the next three in the selection – are all saying the same thing really, the effect of Tebbit telling people to get on their bike and all that fucking nonsense.

CONFESSIONS OF A POP GROUP (1988)

Cheap and tacky bullshit land
Told when to sit, don't know where you stand
Too busy recreating the past to live in the future

Poor relation to Uncle Sam
Bears no relation to the country, man
Too busy being someone else to be who you really are

Shitty plastic prefab town
Mind where you walk when the sun goes down
Too busy hating others to even love your own

Bobbies on the beat again
Beating blacks for blues again
It's one way to get involved in the community

Love me, love my jeans
I must buy shares in Heinz baked beans
Too busy buying up, selling out, selling off

3,2,1, in others' terms
Win a life sentence and a Queen Mum perm
The individual's the state in a state of siege

Do pop and press and mix, do tits and news stew
The next one in the poor house could be you
Too busy saying 'thank you' to say what for?

No time to spare – spare me a dime?
The great depression is organised crime
Their confessions are written in your blood

Kiss your ass and dreams goodbye
Come back when you've learnt to cry
Too busy trying to be strong to see how weak you are

Wave your flags and waive your fate
The freedom you claim is the one you hate
The victory you seek will never come

Brutal views through brutal eyes
See no future, hear no lies
Speak no truth to me or the people I love

When I grow up I want to be
All the things you've never been
And your opinion will count for none

... still America's lapdog, still jumping every time they shout. What's changed?

LIFE AT A TOP PEOPLE'S HEALTH FARM (1988)

Dad's gone down the dog track, Engel's laying cables
Brother's with his student friends plotting in the stables
They're preparing for power and how to win
I'm covered in Solaire and preparing to swim
Old iron! Old iron! I heard the bobby shout
As he brought his friendly truncheon down
With a God almighty clout

Mother's playing bingo, she's hoping for a big win
She buys the daily papers to see how ten per cent live
My cousin's greatest wish is to one day buy a farm
And turn it into a health club with top people charm
Any evening, any day, I'm singing to myself,
I'll pack up all my clothes and dough and piss off somewhere else

My ol' man was a dustperson until he got the shove
Now the iron heel he talked about is backed by the iron glove
Brother's bought new glasses, shaped like Leon Trotsky's
They look very nice on the mantelpiece, next to the Royal Family
I'm laying back with the radio on, in time to hear The Archers
An everyday tale of country folk mixed up in prostitution

Like all good stories with a happy end, which I'll now give to you
Our cousin's wish was granted and so his dream came true
His gas shares doubled while his telecoms soared
'Til he had enough money to chair his own board
And thank you Margaret Thatcher, may you never come to harm
He now serves cocktails and lettuce at a top people's health club farm

There's an old Joe Brown cockney knees-up song I had in mind – 'dad's gone down the dog track etc.'. I started from there and put a contemporary twist on it. The iron heel is a reference to the Jack London book and there's also a reference to Jeffery Archer in there, the everyday tale of country folk...

A STONE'S THROW AWAY (1985)

For liberty there is a cost –
it's broken skulls and leather cosh
From the boys in uniform
Now you know whose side they're on
With backing, with blessing
From earthly gods, not heaven
A stone's throw away from it all

Whatever pleasures those who get
From stripping skin with rhino whip
Are the kind that must be stopped
Before their kind take all we've got
With loving, with caring
They take great pride in working
The stone's throw away from it all

Whenever honesty persists
You'll hear the snap of broken ribs
Of anyone who'll take no more
Of the lying bastard's roar
In Chile
In Poland
Johannesburg
South Yorkshire
A stone's throw away
– now we're there

At the time it seemed whenever you turned on the news there was a policeman smashing someone on the head with a stick somewhere in the world. And then it was happening in Britain as well. One minute the miners were the nation's heroes, bravely digging our coal, the backbone of the nation; the next they were filthy red scum.

ENGLISH ROSE (1978)

No matter where I roam
I will come back to my English rose
For no bonds can ever tempt me from she

I've sailed the seven seas
I've flown the whole blue sky
But I've returned with haste
To where my love does lie

No matter where I go
I will come back to my English rose
For nothing can ever tempt me from she

I've searched the secret mists
I've climbed the highest peaks
Caught the wild wind home
To hear her soft voice speak

No matter where I roam
I will return to my English rose
For no bonds can ever keep me from she

I've been to ancient worlds
I've scoured the whole universe
And caught the first train home
To be at her side

No matter where I roam
I will return to my English rose
For no bonds can ever keep me from she

Written in America on one our early tours. A love song, obviously. But it was also me being homesick, missing England in a place that seemed so strange and unreal.

PARIS MATCH (1983)

Empty hours spent combing the street
In daytime showers, they've become my beat
As I walk from café to bar, I wish I knew where you are
Because you've clouded my mind
And now I'm all out of time

Empty skies say try to forget
Better advice is to have no regrets
As I tread the boulevard floor, will I see once more?
Because you've clouded my mind
'til then I'm biding my time

Empty nights with nothing to do
I sit and think, every thought is for you
I get so restless and bored. So I go out once more
I hate to feel so confined
I feel like I'm wasting my time

I'm only sad in a natural way
And I enjoy sometimes feeling this way
The gift you gave is desire
The match that started my fire

I was going through my heavy French phase, so this was my attempt at a torch song, a Style Council *chanson.*

NOW THE NIGHT IS HERE (2002)

Let's you and I blow gently on the embers of today
Now the night is here to tell us
To be in love

Let us not talk harshly now, our time is to reconcile
Now the night is here to tell us
To be in love

Now the night softly says
That the world is here to stay
Falling out of misty dreams
We arrive so swift it seems to me

No velvet dress can compare to your beauty
Face so fair
And your grace shall carry you through
To a better place
And I shall follow you
And be in love

Let's cast the wind that brought us here 'til we know not when
Now the night is here to tell us
To be in love

It's after one of those awful domestics; now it's the time to heal.

UP IN SUZE'S ROOM (1997)

Yellow strands mingle into red
Warm air blows down upon her soft bed
She licks my face and the feeling spreads
I'm up in Suze's room, flowers bloom in full
I'm up in Suze's room, where life goes so soon

She's everything that you can call free
She's everything that she wants to be
She has everything that you could want to see
I'm up in Suze's room, flowers bloom in full
I'm up in Suze's room, where time goes so soon

Soon, beneath the moon, a big sky paints
But she calls the tunes
She's cool that way, and how I wish I could stay
Forever that way

No one moves, no one can
When luck rolls its coins, they land where you stand
To make us everything that you never planned
I'm up in Suze's room, people bloom in full
Up in Suze's room, where life goes so soon

You can find yourself with strangers in the strangest of places sometimes, but that doesn't make the moment any less beautiful. I've always believed that good luck places you in amazing settings.

ALL ON A MISTY MORNING (2005)

I come to you when you least expect
I call to you to come with me now
I ask of you to drop all things, of absolution
And whatever may be in your hands

All on a misty morning
I come to you with love
All on a misty morning
I come to you
I come to you
with love

I talk to you as a lover should
With a voice close to your ear
If I may get so near enough
You might hear what I hear

It was all on a misty morning
I come to you with love
All on a misty morning
I come to you
I come to you
with love

Let my hands be nimble, let my tongue be quick
Let my loins move slowly against your skin
Let my face and mind disappear for a while
Let my kisses rain down like silk
Let our spit and sweat mingle into one
Let it form a stream of union
That would always run
Forever on
And would have no start and know no end
And would have no start and know no end

All on a misty morning
I come to you with love

The age of romance ... maybe dead, but not necessarily the art.

MONDAY (1980)

Oh baby, I'm dreaming of Monday
Oh baby, will I see you again
Oh baby, I'm dreaming of Monday

Rainclouds came and stole my thunder
Left me barren like a desert
But a sunshine girl like you
It's worth going through
I will never be embarrassed about love again

Tortured winds that blew me over
When I start to think that I'm something special
They tell me that I'm not
And they're right and I'm glad and I'm not
I will never be embarrassed about that again

Oh baby, I'm dreaming of Monday
Oh baby, will I see you again
Oh baby, I'm dreaming of Monday

The challenge was to write a love song about the least romantic day of the week. I like the Englishness of this lyric – the weekend's over, this character is having to go back to work but is so in love that they can't wait to see the other person again. It could be an office romance.

THE BITTEREST PILL (1982)

In your white lace and your wedding bells
You look the picture of contented new wealth
But from the on-looking fool who believed your lies
I wish this grave would open up and swallow me alive
For the bitterest pill is hard to swallow
The love I gave hangs in sad-coloured mocking shadows

When the wheel of fortune broke you fell to me
Out of grey skies to change my misery
The vacant spot, your beating heart took its place
But now I watch smoke leave my lips and fill an empty room
For the bitterest pill is hard to swallow
The love I gave hangs in sad coloured mocking shadows

The bitterest pill is mine to take
If I took if for a hundred years I couldn't feel anymore ill

Now autumn's breeze blows summer leaves through my life
Twisted and broken down, no days with sunlight
The dying spark, you left your mark on me
The promise of your kiss – but with someone else
For the bitterest pill is mine to swallow
The love I gave hangs in sad coloured mocking shadows

The bitterest pill is mine to take
If I took if for a hundred years I couldn't feel anymore ill

Another attempt to write a three-minute Play For Today.

PRECIOUS (1982)

Your precious love, it means so much
Will it ever stop or will I just lose touch
What I want to say, but my words just fail
Is that I need it so, I can't help myself
Like a hungry child I just help myself
And when I'm all full up I go out to play

But I don't mean to bleed you dry
Or take you over for the rest of your life
It's just that I need something solid in mine

Lonely as the moors on a winter's morning
Quiet as the sea on a cool calm night
In your tranquil shadow, I try and follow
I hear your distant shoe clicks to the midnight beat
I feel trapped in sorrow, in this imagery
But that's how I am and why I need you so

LOVE-LESS (2000)

Midnight star
Light the way
For thoughts that change
Like night to day
And bless the course
That runs in time
No matter how far
Shine my way!

I've got a need to be loved
Yes I want to be loved
I've got a need to be loved
Like anyone else

Bring the night
Go bring all your thunder
Nearer the light
Shine here amongst us
No matter the flight
Fill me with wonder

Another of my songs about God. Written at a low time and looking for a sign.

YOU DO SOMETHING TO ME (1995)

You do something to me
something deep inside
I'm hanging on the wire
for love I'll never find
You do something wonderful
and chase it all away
Mixing my emotions
that throw me back again

Hanging on the wire
I'm waiting for the change
I'm dancing through the fire
Just to catch a flame
      to feel real again

You do something to me
somewhere deep inside
Hoping to get close to
a peace I cannot find

Dancing through the fire
just to catch a flame
just to get close to
just close enough to tell you that –

You do something to me
something deep inside

This definitely strikes a chord in people's hearts, a song for lovers. I'm told by so many people they had it played at their wedding, the first dance … Ironically, it's really about unattainable love. But you can interpret it whichever way you want.

I SHOULD HAVE BEEN THERE TO INSPIRE YOU (1997)

Nothing I would say or I could do
Could move the mountains from your view
Nothing I would see or I could show
There's only darkness now I know
I should have been there to inspire you
Not paint your world a cold, cold blue
I should have been there to inspire you
I could have told you, truthful too
I believed in you

I should have been there within your reach
This is not self pity of which I speak

I never took time to see you grow
I never took the care it takes to know
Never took the time to see what you'd found
But always had the time to bring you down

More than all this, I do not know
Only that love is here to show
Someone a world, to be themselves
A place to fall when all else fails
And friends' harsh words cut deep and sore
But believe me mine will hurt me more
In those moments before I sleep
When I am truly alone to see

I should have been there to inspire you
Not paint your world a cold, cold blue
I should have been there to inspire you
I could have told you, truthful too
That I believed in you

A YEAR LATE (1995)

Something worn like a blanket from
your tender heart, your crystal spirit
Keeps me warm and safe from harm
Wrapped around my shoulders

I love to wake and watch your face
And while you sleep I fall for you again
Is it true, what I feel for you
Wish I could help it through
So you could feel it too

And the leaves around the door
And the sunlight in the hall
And the darkness that will fall
Make me want you more

Morning breaks on the icy flakes
that collect around our window
The cold outside is a harsh goodbye
Clouds at our mouths as we breath a sigh

And as I look, like a unending book
Page after page, you are turning
Is it true what I feel for you
Wish I could help it through
So you could feel it too

And the leaves around my door
And the sunlight in the hall
And the darkness that will fall
Just make me want you more

TIME PASSES (1995)

I saw you today or at least I think it was
It's hard to say, we've all changed so much
Compelled to look but I hid my face
It's hard to trace these feelings

Gone so soon the time I spent with you
Like an old, old tune, keeps running through my head
I wanted to say so many things
But my mouth went dry and one word and I'd cry

Slender bride, your beauty shines from you
And forever more I'll be on your side for sure
A light in your life that always burns for you
As time passes so quickly

The final stage we've both reached some way
As we board our trains to different stations
And the parts we play and the things we say
Words on the way to discovery

A story set on Kensington High Street.

DUST AND ROCKS (2000)

Well she's waiting by the window
Worth a fading tear
That will slip in to tomorrow
And have no fear
She may look back and blame you
But you only blame yourself
And what good would it all do you
If you thought she blamed herself

It's a lonely life, as bits of dust and rocks
When you shake it off it's all you have
In the time it takes to find another space
Get to live again
She'll run and run –
Still she's waiting by the window
With a fading tear

Well she looks upon high flying silver dreams
How she wishes how
She could climb aboard
never coming back
Turn on it all

Find another space, learn to live again
Find the other parts of little planets that are
Coursing through your veins
Bits of dust and rocks
No need to shake them off -
she'll run and run
Still she's waiting by the window
She has no fear

We're all just particles of dust, cooling down, reshaping, resolving. There are two levels to this lyric – the woman left alone contemplating her future and then the cosmic stuff, the bigger picture, and her place in all that too.

MOON ON YOUR PYJAMAS (1993)

Was that a shooting star I saw?
It's rare for me to make a wish at all
Because I feel that I can only hope
These dangerous times, we are barely afloat

I hope the world will heal itself
And our worn out souls along with it
So that you will get the chance to say
You have seen a better day

You've got the moon on your pyjamas
And the stars in your eyes
Sweet child you're a dream in disguise
Angels on silver strings hang from above
Let love and laughter shine wherever you go

Through your new eyes I've come to see
How beautiful my life can be
And I'll keep this wish this time I think
And blow it in with a kiss upon your head

And I hope the world will heal itself
And our worn out souls along with it
So that you will get the chance to see
A summer's blue sky behind green trees

You've got the moon on your pyjamas
And the stars in your eyes
Sweet child you're a dream in disguise
Angels on silver strings hang from above
Let love and laughter shine wherever you go

A lullaby written for and about my first-born child, Nat.

SWEET PEA, MY SWEET PEA (2000)

Sweet pea, my sweet pea
You're the one to get my heart a-jumpin'
Light of love all around your being to see

The future, it's looking at you
It only exists because you're alive
So close your eyes and smile
your smiles of sweet dreams
And fill them with love again
Sweet pea
Fill them with joy again

Each pace I take, you know why
I write for you and I too try
To take the things that lie around
And turn them into dreams so swift, so proud
It's on time again
And it's mine again

Sweet thing, loving you is easy
Goodbye sadness when I'm around you
Giving me something I can feel down in my bones

Ah, sometimes, maybe just sometimes
Look back on these times and smile
And have the grace to know
What you have seen

And fill 'em with love again

Sweet pea
You fill me with hope again!
My Sweet Pea

Recollected thoughts and songs
Emblems of forgotten words
Remnants of a time so clear
That still rings fresh and true
When the wind is here
It's on time again
And it's mine again!

Sweet pea, my sweet pea
Heaven knows I got a thing about you
You're the girl to get my heart
Start jumpin' again

Ah, sometimes, baby just sometimes
Look back on these times and smile
And have the grace to know
What you have seen

How it should be, my sweet pea
Only God knows what I feel about you
You're the girl to get my heart
Start pumpin' around

The future? Its looking at you.
It only exists because you're alive
So close your eyes and smile
Your smiles of sweet dreams...

And fill 'em with love again

This was dedicated to Leah, but it's about all my kids, they're all branches of the same tree.

FLY ON THE WALL (1992)

Where angels meet
Their words are whispers
As sea touches shore
The clouds move swiftly
And me, so small
Compared to it all
Like a fly on the wall

As pieces sweep
Their meaning is still no clearer
And under my feet
There's nothing to stop my own free fall
Down and down I go
And compared to it all
I'm a fly on the wall

Our children sleep
Resting our hopes and wishes
The night in between
I'm casting my scope, just fishing
And in spite of it all
Oh, I look at me so small
And compared to it all
I'm a fly on the wall

I wrote this sitting on a beach, imagining I could see myself from out in space, see myself as a speck of sand. The strange way we are all integral to the world but the paradox of how transient we are too.

WINGS OF SPEED (1995)

Fly on wings of speed
That will bring you home to me
I'll never be free from the darkness I see
As I wait for your smile

Though my hands are tied
My feet are bound by fate
With clay at the base as I sit and wait
What visions I see

In dreams she floats on a stream
With Jesus at the helm
The water reeds that beg
her boat along the way
As she comes to me

Now as the light is falling
One candle left to light the way
Sailing home to morning
She comes to me calling
To brighten up my darkest day
And the world fades away with her smile

Fly on wings of speed
That will bring you home to me
I'll never be free from the darkness I see
As I wait for your smile

I wrote this about The Lady Of Shalott *by John William Waterhouse. I tried to evoke what I saw in this brilliant painting, though why we are moved by art remains a mystery to me. A beautiful mystery that I never want answered.*

ROLL ALONG SUMMER (2005)

Roll along summer
Whispering thru' my window pane
Wake me up and whole again
         with a sway

Skate upon something
Get me up and out of bed
Put a volt right thru' my head
         and beyond

You've been down and out and blue
Take no notice of the moon
         shame

Ol' man river's after you
Said you ain't done what you said y'would
         it's a shame
         shame

Roll along summer
Breathing life into the world
Creating space that wasn't there before

Forever in your shadows
It's a darkness I can face
Proud to feel I find a place
         somewhere behind

You've been down and out and blue
Take no notice of the moon
                    shame
Ol' man river's after you
Said you ain't done what you said y'would
                    it's a shame
                    shame

Roll along, beautiful lover
Show me things I've never seen
Lighting up an ancient beam
                    for me to see

It's a hymn to summer coming and with it love and excitement and the thrill of life anew.

MY EVER CHANGING MOODS (1983)

Daylight turns to moonlight and I'm at my best
Praising the way it all works and gazing upon the rest
The cool before the warm, the calm after the storm
The cool before the warm, the calm after the storm
I wish to stay forever, letting this be my food
But I'm caught up in a whirlwind and my ever changing moods

Bitter turns to sugar, some call a passive tune
But the day things turn sweet for me won't be too soon
The hush before the silence, the winds after the blast
The hush before the silence, the winds after the blast
I wish we'd move together, this time the bosses sued
But we're caught up in the wilderness and an ever changing mood

Teardrops turn to children who've never had the time
To commit the sins they pay for through another's evil mind
The love after the hate, the love we leave too late
The love after the hate, the love we leave too late
I wish we'd wake up one day and everyone feel moved
But we're caught up in the dailies and an ever changing mood

Evil turns to statues and masses form a line
But I know which way I'd run to if the choice was mine
The past is knowledge, the present our mistake
And the future we always leave too late
I wish we'd come to our senses and see there is no truth
In those who promote the confusion of this ever changing mood

On one level, this is about my own moods, which were probably even more dramatic at that time. I've slowed down in my old age. But it's also reflecting some of the pressing concerns of the day – the ever present threat of The Bomb and the mad tyrants. We'd been down to Greenham Common around this time to deliver some food and clothes to the women. A fucking scary place to be.

THE CHANGINGMAN (1995)

Is happiness real or am I so jaded?
I can't see or feel, like a man been tainted
Numbed by the effect, aware of the muse
Too in touch with myself
I light the fuse!

I'm the changingman, built on shifting sands
I'm the changingman, waiting for the bang
As I light a bitter fuse

Time is on loan, only ours to borrow
What I can't be today, I can be tomorrow
And the more I see, the more I know
The more I know, the less I understand

I'm the changingman, built on shifting sands
I'm the changingman, waiting for the bang
As I light a bitter fuse

It's a bigger part
When our instincts act
A shot in the dark
A movement in black

And the more I see, the more I know
The more I know, the less I understand
I'm the changingman, built on shifting sands
I'm the changingman, waiting for the bang
As I light a bitter fuse

Autobiography, written during another period of great change for me. My fortunes were rising once again but I was also splitting up with my wife. It's about me needing to mix up the puzzle just when things are falling into place, set fire to it, light the fuse. And then try to put it back together again, awkwardly.

It started with the title, which came from my daughter, Leah – she was playing with a little doll and I said 'who's this then?' She said 'it's the changingman'.

ABOVE THE CLOUDS (1992)

Autumn blew its leaves at me
Threatening winter as I walked
Summer always goes so quick
Barely stopping like my thoughts
Which dip and spin and change so fast
I have to wonder
– will I last?

Through the windows of the train
I caught reflections of a paper cup
Hanging small in a pale blue sky
Never knowing which way's up

Above the clouds, what's to be found
I have to wonder
– will I be around?

As my anger shouts at my old self doubt
So a sadness creeps into my dreams
When you're scared of living but afraid to die
I get scared of giving
And I must find the faith to beat it

It must be me that's rushing by
Time just lingers on the wind
Bristling through my open fears
I wonder what it's going to bring

Above the clouds, what's to be found
I have to wonder
– will I be around?

Run and hide, run and hide
I catch the sail at evening's tide

At the time of writing this lyric, I wasn't sure whether I wanted to even play music any-more or whether people wanted to hear it anyway. I'd stopped completely... just a crisis of confidence really.

HAVE YOU EVER HAD IT BLUE? (1986)

Have you ever chased the night that sailed in front of you
On a boat that was bound for hope but left you in the queue
With your shouting, waving, taunting, flaunting friends as crew
Telling you that every lie you ever heard was true
Have you stood upon that deck
Have you ever had it blue?

Have you ever woken to find the morning didn't come
Undelivered with the papers, stolen by someone
Found the milkman bound 'n gagged and shackles round the sun
And the holder of the keys turns out to be the one
The girl you had your heart set on
Have you ever had it blue?

Have you ever watched the day passing by your door
Powerless to change its course, your feet fixed to the floor
When all the people you thought you knew are changing more and more
Even the girl you thought would see seems only to ignore
The only love worth fighting for
Have you ever had it blue?

This is one of the only lyrics I've ever been commissioned to write, for the film of Absolute Beginners. *Brilliant book by Colin McInnes, shit film, unfortunately. It was an interesting challenge to have to write to a brief, though.*

IT'S A VERY DEEP SEA (1988)

I'll keep on diving 'til I reach the ends
Dredging up the past to drive me round the bends
What is it in me that I can't forget?
I keep finding so much that I now regret
But no, on I go down into the depths
Turning things over that are better left
Dredging up the past that has gone for good
Trying to polish up what is rotting wood

Diving
I'm diving, diving

Something inside takes me down again
Diving not for goblets but tin cans
Dredging up the past for reasons so rife
Passing bits of wrecks that once passed for life
But I'll keep on diving till I drown the sea
of things not worth even mentioning
Perhaps I'll come to the surface and come to my senses
But it's a very deep sea around my own devices

Diving
I'm diving, diving

A lyric which takes it's cue from the nature of the chords, which were influenced by Debussy and Satie, who I was listening to a lot. I've got a fixation with the sea anyway, but I think we all have, it's where we're from.

DOWN IN THE SEINE (1985)

Catch me I'm falling so fast and I can't seem to find
All the reasons I had when the purpose was mine
Now I stumble so fast rolling into the night
Kiss me quick before I land and am broken in two
Keep me on the right track, hold my dreams intact too
I get lost in this place, I get lost, yes it's true

Quand on na plus rien en soi, quand on na plus de refuge
Quand on ne peut plus fuir, quand on ne sais on courir
Noir comme la nuit, oui, noir comme mon ame
Noir comme les eaux, dans lesquels je sombre

Help me I'm sinking so fast into waters unplanned
That I once held onto but have got out of hand
Now the things that I loved are the things I can't stand
Squeeze me slow before I come to that part of the ground
It's a million miles up and a million miles down
I get lost in between and I wait to be found

And in the waters I sink and in the waters I drink
Until I rise to the top, which in truth it is not
It's the same as below, so let's put on a show
To make you feel you're alright, to make you feel there's no fight

Catch me I'm falling so fast

A lot of the lyrics are littered with little in-jokes, just for me really. The kiss me quick, squeeze me slowly; I liked the reference to the English seaside holiday amidst a supposedly more glamourous and romantic setting.

IT JUST CAME TO PIECES IN MY HANDS (1983)

I stood as tall as a mountain
I never really thought about the drop
I trod over rocks to get there
Just so I could stand on top
Clumsy and blind I stumbled
As I crawled through desert sands
I didn't stop to think about the consequences
As it came to pieces in my hands

I thought I was a maritime marvel
I believed that I ruled the waves
All I could say was time is motion
And every effort others made I would save
I was a shit stained statue
School children would stand in awe
I truly believed I was a ceiling of the sky
Never thought about having flaws

I felt as reverent as Jesus
The sanctimony stunk
I thought I was admiral of the missing fleet
I couldn't see that I was sunk
I roared my pride in the darkness
I scratched away at the stars
I thought I was lord of this crappy jungle
I should have been put behind bars

But now I sit with my head in my hands
And wail to the weeping wall
The avalanche of my emotions
Holds the audience of one enthralled
Like learning the lesson the hard way
Like a fall from command
I thought I was king of the whole wide world
But it just came to pieces in my hands

The following section of four lyrics all deal with the breaking down of idols, ego, self-obsession. This one speaks for itself.

PORCELAIN GODS (1995)

Beware false prophets – take a stand!
My fortune cookie cracked up in my hand
More advice to fill up your head
More empty words from the living dead
Who seek to explain what can't really be said
And how disappointed I was
To turn out after all
Just a porcelain god
    that shatters when it falls

Too much will kill you, too little ain't enough
You shout my name but I'll call your bluff
Most who see me see me not for real
We fake and fawn, play games 'til dawn
But I can see what you can see
And I hate too what you hate in me
How disappointed I am
To find me part of no plan
Just a porcelain god
    that shatters when it falls

I shake it off and start again
Don't lose control, I tell myself
Life can take many things away
Some people will try to take it all
They'll pick off pieces as they watch you crawl
And how disappointed I was
To turn out after all
Just a porcelain god
that shatters when it falls

     that shatters when it falls

This has that air of paranoid druggy menace and it's about fame on one level and personal ego on another. I had this image of a small plaster Buddha toppling from the mantelpiece and shattering on the floor.

CARNATION (1982)

If you gave me a fresh carnation
I would only crush its tender petals
With me you'll have no escape
And at the same time there'll be nowhere to settle
I trample down all life in my wake
I eat it up and take the cake
I just avert my eyes to the pain
Of someone's loss helping my gain

If you gave me a dream for my pocket
You'd be plugging in the wrong socket
With me there's no room for the future
With me there's no room with a view at all
I am out of season all year round
Hear machinery roar to my empty sound
Touch my heart and feel winter
Hold my hand and be doomed forever

If you gave me a fresh carnation
I would only crush its tender petals
With me you'll have no escape
And at the same time there'll be nowhere to settle
And if you're wondering by now who I am
Look no further than the mirror
Because I am the Greed and Fear
And every ounce of Hate in you

A lot of my songs are about me. This one's about you.

GHOSTS (1981)

Why are you frightened, can't you see that it's you
That ain't no ghost, it's a reflection of you
Why do you turn away, keep it out of sight
Oh, don't live up to your given roles
There's more inside you that you won't show
But you keep it hidden just like everyone
Too scared to show you care, it'll make you vulnerable
So you wear that ghost around you for disguise
But there's no need, just 'cos it's all we've known
There's more inside you that you haven't shown
So keep on movin', movin', movin' your feet
Keep on shuf-shuf-shuffling to this ghost dance beat
Just keep on walking down never-ending streets
One day you'll walk right out of this life
And then you'll wonder why you didn't try
To spread some loving all around
Old fashioned causes like that still stand
Gotta rid this prejudice that ties you down
How do you feel at the end of the day
Just like you've walked over your own grave –
So why are you frightened, can't you see that it's you
At the moment there's nothing so there's nothing to lose
Lift up your lonely heart and walk right on through

I was trying to call out to my generation, a rallying call in the name of inspiration and fulfilment.

BRAND NEW START (1998)

I'm gonna clear out my head
I'm gonna get myself straight
I know it's never too late
To make a brand new start

I'm gonna kick down the door
I'm gonna get myself in
I'm gonna fix up the yard
And not fall back again

I'm gonna clean up my earth
And build a heaven on the ground
Not something distant and unfound
But something real to me

All that I can I can be
All that I am I can see
All that is mine is in my hands
So to myself I call

There's somewhere else I should be
There's someone else I can see
There's something more I can find
It's only up to me

I'm gonna clean up my earth
And build a heaven on the ground
Not something distant and unfound
But something real to me

I'm gonna clear out my head
I'm gonna get myself straight
I know it's never too late
To make a brand new start

I remember trying to finish this in time to play it at a benefit concert we were doing for Shelter. *It's a simple message: whatever's broken in life is there for the fixing.*

HAS MY FIRE REALLY GONE OUT? (1993)

And if I open my eyes, will it then be morning?
First rays of summer sun coming down and shining
And if I open my heart and say all that you would want
Hold faith and all I believe
Will be there to greet me

Put an end to all your doubts
Has my fire really gone out?

And if I open my head, remember all that I said
Hey baby, what will you find coming down to meet you –
A lot of words but no one talking
I don't want no part of that
Something real is what I'm seeking
One clear voice in the wilderness

Put an end to all your doubts
Has my fire really really gone out?

There's an ironic twist to this. I was coming out of my wilderness years and there were those who were wondering whether I still had it, whether my fire had gone out. But I knew I hadn't and I'd sing this with a smile.

INTO TOMORROW (1991)

Into the mists of time and space
Where we have no say over date and place
Don't get embarrassed that it happens a lot
That you don't know how you started or where you're gonna stop

And if at times it seems insane, all the tears and searching
Turning all your joy to pain in pursuit of learning
Buy a dream and hideaway, can't escape the sorrow
Your mojo will have no effect as we head
into tomorrow

Round and round like a twisted wheel
Spinning in attempt to find the feel
Find the path that will help us find
A feeling of control over lives and minds

And if at times it seems insane, all the tears and searching
Turning all your joy to pain in pursuit of learning
Buy a dream and hideaway, can't escape the sorrow
Your mojo will have no effect – as we head
into tomorrow

Into the stars and always up
Drinking from a broken cup
Whose golden gleam is fading fast
Praying that it has not passed
into tomorrow

Hitting my thirties was both confusing and exciting, a world of new possibilities. Here I was posing the big questions: where are we from, where are we going etc. ... and yet I still managed to work in a few mod references. The Twisted Wheel and the Mojo were both big Northern Soul clubs in Manchester and Sheffield in the 60s. It's my nod to them and their legacy.

SCIENCE (1997)

I have my thoughts to position but do I know how to act?
I have no silent ambitions but does that make me a man?
Until I learn all I can and mean all I understand
as a way of giving

And I'm a piece of the earth, I take no offence
I can be who I am, I have no pretence
Only to what you can be, if you want to be
It's a way of living

I've got a pen in my pocket, does that make me a writer?
Standing on the mountain doesn't make me no higher
Putting on gloves don't make you a fighter
And all the study in the world doesn't make it science

So grab a piece in the air, try to make it sing
Try and be who you can, it's the real, real thing
I'm into what you can be if you want to be
It's a way of living

I've got a pick in my pocket, does that make me a player?
Words can't do what action does louder
Putting on gloves don't make you a fighter
And all the study in the world doesn't make it science

I've got a pen in my pocket, does that make me a writer?
Standing on the mountain doesn't make me no higher
Putting on gloves don't make you a fighter
And all the study in the world doesn't make it science

Some things are unexplainable, however much scientific knowledge we have, and I think we should rejoice in that. You can't chart every inch of the world.

The reference to boxing was for my dad who fought for England ABA. The sweet science.

AS YOU LEAN INTO THE LIGHT (1997)

Gentle rain, here it comes again
Rattling 'round your window, threatening pain
Coming on like a friend that you know better than
yesterday that held you by a different hand

Hail and stone and all that's gone
When everything that passes cuts to the bone
Turning like a wheel dragging a heavy stone
A weight that ties you down, that you will never own

Strange to see a paper smile on thee
When once you moved and lit the room for us all to see
Now if I could be the sun I'd shine in your life
If I could be the rain I'd fall from your eyes
And I'd wash away the emptiness you feel inside

*I wrote this for a friend who was going through a rough time. The title suggests that,
though leaning into the light you may become clearer, the shadows you cast fill the room
with other complexities*

FOOT OF THE MOUNTAIN (1993)

Like a dream on the ocean, always drifting away
And I can't catch up, she just skips away on the tide
Sometimes a great notion can lead you astray
So weak to devotion, so strong to desire

Baby, won't you let me ride
Take me off on your sail boat ride
Come on now, angels are on your side
But she slips away
and never stays

Like mercury gliding, a silver teardrop that falls
And I can't hold on, through my fingers she's gone
At the foot of the mountain, such a long way to climb
How will I ever get up there?
– though I know I must try

Like a dream on the ocean, always drifting away
And I can't catch up, she just skips away on the tide
She just slips away on the tide
Skips away as she glides

Very rarely is a song totally autobiographical. For me, writing is often just about coming up with words, images, situations that I hope people will connect to. That's sometimes enough for me.

HUNG UP (1994)

Hidden in the back seat of my head
Some place I can't remember where
I found it just by coincidence
And now I'm all hung up again

Just like a soldier from the past
Who won't be told it's over yet
Refusing to lay down his gun
He'll keep on fighting 'til his war is won
He's just gotta hurt someone
He'll keep on fighting 'til his war is won

Waiting for the moment
That will catch me with surprise
Extraordinary, trying to cease the war inside

Hidden in the back seat of my head
Some place I can't remember where
I found it just by coincidence
An' now I'm all hung up again

There comes a time when you have to go with the changes and give up chasing your demons. Move off and let them chase you.

BULL-RUSH (1992)

In a momentary lapse of my condition
That sent me tumbling down into a deep despair
Lost and dazed so I had no real recollection
Until the rain cleared the air

When you wake to find that everything has left you
And the clothes you wear belong to someone else
See your shadow chasing off towards the shore line
Drifting into emptiness

There are bullrushes outside my window
And their leaves whisper words in the breeze
Tomorrow I'll walk to the harbour
And catch the first boat that's coming in

Like a child too small to reach the front door handle
Maybe just too scared to know what I would find
Now I feel I'm strong enough to take the slow ride
Not knowing when I will arrive

I do believe I'm going home
'cause I don't call this place my own
I'm missing what I had
    happy times and sad
More than I ever thought could be

There are bullrushes outside my window
And their leaves whisper words in the breeze
Tomorrow I'll walk to the harbour
And catch the first boat that's coming in

Written when I was recording my first solo LP. There really were bullrushes outside the window where I was staying, the wind whistled through the leaves like voices. There are signs in life that you can choose either to brush off or take notice of. I'm a believer.

ILLUMINATION (2002)

I close my eyes
but sleep won't come
You're in my waking dreams
It's a feeling right inside of me
'til you're in my arms again

The prayer I ask
Is where I'm going to
Without your undying love
I'm as worthless as a cold, cold sun
That shines for no one at all

How many time must I return
From distant oceans just to learn
That with your song
Illumination comes

I close my ears
And I hear no one
I'm in a moving film
It's black and white and beautiful
and it has no end to write

I tried to write this as a prayer; it could be to a lover, a loved one or God, I'm never quite sure myself. Perhaps it's all three, another variation on the Holy Trinity

FRIGHTENED (2000)

I shake and fall underneath my sheets
The sunlight creeping from my head down to my feet
Telling me to rise and face the light again
I plead to dawn – don't make me move –
I just want to vanish and forget all that's true
Just one more night and I'll be alright

Hoping to be everything you want
Wish I was the man you thought I was
Waiting to fly up on eagle's wings
But truth be told, I'm not that bold at all
I'm more frightened
White lightning, so sudden and blinding
Yet no more enlightened
Just a little more frightened

I'm gonna get it back, I'm gonna get it soon
I've just got to catch up for my world to resume
To be light and to hold you tight while you dream
And I stand alone, so does everyone
It brings us closer together as a strange distant sun
So near, so far, like distant stars

Hoping to be everything you want
Wish I was the man that you thought I was
Waiting to fly up on eagle's wings
But truth be told, I'm not that bold at all
I'm just frightened
Woke up this morning like that
And all the roads that lead back
Lead me to nothing that is nowhere –
lonely –
And just a little more frightened
White lightning
So sudden and blinding
Yet no more enlightened
Just a little more frightened

The morning after the night before … and still no wiser.

WOODCUTTER'S SON (1995)

Sugartown has turned so sour
Its people angry in their sleep
There's more small-town paranoia
Sweeping down in evil sheets

You can tell it's witching hour
You can feel the spirits rise
When the room goes very quiet
And there's hatred in their eyes

There's a silence when I enter
And a murmur when I leave
I can see their jealous faces
I can feel the ice they breathe

You better give me the chance
I'll cut you down with a glance
With my small axe, so help me
And though I'm only one
And though weak, I'm strong
But if push comes to shove
Then I'm the woodcutter's son

I'm cutting down the wood
For the good of everyone

The title comes directly from reading fairy tales to my kids. But I applied it to the idea of fame and paranoia. Be careful what you wish for because it might come and cut yer head off...

PEACOCK SUIT (1996)

I've got a grapefruit matter
It's as sour as shit
I have no solutions
– better get used to it!

I don't need a ship to sail in stormy weather
I don't need you to ruffle the feathers of my Peacock Suit

I'm Narcissus in a puddle
In shop windows I gloat
Like a ball of fleece lining
In my camel skin coat

I don't need a ship to sail in stormy weather
I don't need you to ruffle the feathers of my Peacock Suit

I'm Nemesis in a muddle
In a mirror I look
Like a streak of sheet lightning
In my rattlesnake shoes

I don't need a ship to sail in stormy weather
I don't need you to ruffle the feathers of my Peacock Suit
– did you think I should?

I liked the idea of casting these classical Greek characters in the everyday setting – Narcissus walking down the high street, Nemesis not knowing who to blame, who to seek retribution from. The camel skin coat is just a daft joke about getting the hump. It made me laugh anyway … It's harder to get away with writing an 'angry song' when you're older (I would have been thirty-eight, thirty-nine when I wrote this). This is the difference between between being an angry young man and a miserable old git.

ABSOLUTE BEGINNERS (1981)

In echoed steps I walked across an empty dream
I looked across this world, there was no one to be seen
This empty feeling turned and quietly walked away
I saw no warmth in life, no love was in my eyes

I stared a century, thinking this will never change
As I hesitated time rushed onwards without me
Too scared to break the spell, too small to take a fall
But the absolute luck is
Love is in our hearts

I lost some hours thinking of it
I need the strength to go and get what I want
I lost a lifetime thinking of it
And lost an era daydreaming like I do

In echoed steps you walk across an empty dream
But look around this world, there's millions to be seen
Come see the tyrants panic, see their crumbling empires fall
Then tell 'em we don't fight for fools 'cause
Love is in our hearts

You can lose some hours thinking of it
You need the strength to go and get what you want
You can lose a lifetime thinking of it
And lose an era daydreaming like I do

An attempt to rabble rouse my generation, with a title copped from Colin MacInnes.

THE WEAVER (1993)

Can you put a smile back on all these different faces
Of all these people from such different places
And if you can succeed, what then will you achieve
With a different tune to play you've been saving for a rainy day

Will you heal the scar that's on all the years been wasted
The tears spent on the past, just filling spaces
Or is love forever gone, banished to a smaller part
Hide behind your wall and start to get to the very heart

And if you want to shoot the moon make sure that you know why
Careful, fly too soon, better let someone else try

I'm the weaver of your dreams
I get rid of your bogeyman
I'm here to smash the shell you're under
And get you into another thing
I'm the weaver of your dreams
I put paid to the rocketman
I'm here to break the spell you're under
And get you started with another plan

Could you put a kiss back on the lips so twisted,
Waiting for the chance to start dipping into wishes
Or is love forever gone, banished to a smaller part
Hide behind your wall and start to get to the very heart

And in the midst of the darkest night
Think of me and hold me tight
So that I might live to see
All the weaving of my dreams

I'm the weaver of your dreams
I get rid of your bogeyman
I'm here to smash the shell you're under
And get you into another thing
I'm the weaver of your dreams
I put paid to the rocketman
I'm here to break the spell you're under
And get you started with another plan

*Do all songs have to mean something? Sometimes a meaning springs from the sheer
pleasure of simply putting words together on a page.*

RUNNING ON THE SPOT (1982)

I was hoping we'd make real progress
But it seems we have lost the power
Any tiny step of advancement
Is like a raindrop falling into the ocean
We're running on the spot, always have, always will
We're just the next generation of the emotionally crippled

Though we keep piling up the building blocks
The structure never seems to get any higher
Because we keep kicking out the foundations
And stand useless while our lives fall down
I believe in life and I believe in love
But the world in which I live keeps trying to prove me wrong

Out in the pastures we call society
You can't see further than the bottom of your glass
Only young but easily shocked
You get all violent when the boat gets rocked

Just like sheep, little lambs unto the slaughter
Don't fully grasp what exactly is wrong
Truth is you never cared, still
You get all violent when the boat gets rocked

Intelligence should be our first weapon
Stop revelling in rejection
And follow yourselves not some ageing drain brain
Who's quite content to go on feeding you garbage
We're running on the spot, always have, always will
We're just the next generation of the emotionally crippled

I had such high hopes for my generation, that we'd progress and take the world on some-where new. This lyric carries my sense of disappointment. The Jam had a positive energy that, I think, set us apart from our contemporaries. We always tried to look beyond the simplistic wallowing in rejection. But it's also about myself as well, banging on about the state of the world but unable to get myself out of the pint pot.

BEAT SURRENDER (1982)

Come on boy, come on girl
Succumb to the beat surrender

All the things that I care about are packed into one punch
All the things that I'm not sure about are sorted out at once
And as it was in the beginning, so shall it be in the end
That bullshit is bullshit, it just goes by different names

All the things that I shout about but never act upon
All the courage of the dreams I have, but seem to wait so long
My doubt is cast aside, watch phoneys run to hide
The dignified don't even enter in the game

And if you feel there's no passion, no quality sensation
Seize that young determination, show the fakers you ain't fooling
You'll see me come running to the sound of your strumming
Fill my heart with joy and gladness
I've lived too long in the shadows of sadness

Come on boy, come on girl
Succumb to the beat surrender

Wake me up with an amphetamine blast
Grab me by the collar, throw me out into the world
Rock me gently, send me dreaming soft and tender
I am yours and will always be beholden to
The beat surrender

Not so much a swan song as a fond farewell, an attempt to crystallise all the things The Jam stood for and meant to people. The last part was written as a letter to my audience, 'I am yours …'

COME ON / LET'S GO (2005)

You have never been there 'til you've heard the fat girl sing
Then nothing else matters, everything just pales within
Hanging round the corners, shouting at the top of your voice
Sing you little fuckers, sing like you've got no choice
I believe it's true, we are everywhere
And I feel the wind and it feels so high

There really is no purpose, definitely is no need
To go running round the houses like a racehorse on speed
I believe again, we are everything
And I feel the wind and it gets so high

Come on, baby let's go
You say – where to?
I say I don't know
I just need to run and you need it too
And I catch your eye
And I feel the wind
And it feels so high

We're planting up the acorns, wondering to where they'll lead
We're planting up the acorns, wondering to where they'll seed

Come on, baby let's go
You say – where to?
I say I don't know

The little fuckers are not necessarily the new bands, the next generation. It's not for me to tell them to sing up, that's for them to do, to encourage each other. It's really a song of hope and optimism.

THERE'S NO DRINKING AFTER YOU'RE DEAD (2000)

Come taste the wine, come lose yourself
Take this time but keep it well
Only love it all with heart and head
For there is no drinking after you're dead

Dive and swim in the amber ocean
See all that you can in this new emotion
And embrace it now before its skin sheds
For there is no drinking after you're dead

Stand back to back with yourself again
As you spin and reel like a new found friend
And have it all with heart and hands
For there is no love making after you're dead

And today is but a second if tomorrow you may die
And empty pages glistening in eternity's lie
And time is but an essence encased upon the wall
That brings our day of reckoning much closer to us all

Light the candle and burn it well
For only time knows what it cannot yet tell
Only love it all with heart and head
For there is no drinking after you're dead

I had the Dubliners, Brendan Behan in mind, like an old Irish drinking song.

FROM THE FLOORBOARDS UP (2005)

I've got a feeling from the floorboards up
Call it a calling if you like that touch
Call it what you will
I really don't care too much

I've got a feeling and I know it's right
I get it most evenings, if not every night
It sings in the air
And dances like candlelight

When we play, we play, we play
Mama, from the floorboards up
When we dance, we dance, we dance
Papa, from the floorboards up
When we sway, we sway as one
From the floorboards up
From the floorboards up

I get a feeling from the walls and chairs
They tell me of the things that have always been there
And all that is not
Will have to go back to dust

PAUL WELLER

When we play, we play, we play
Mama, from the floorboards up
When we dance, we dance, we dance
Papa, from the floorboards up
When we sway, we sway as one
From the floorboards up

Playing live on a good night you can feel the energy rising through your body to the ceiling, from the floorboards up. That energy is not just about swinging an arm or smashing a stick on a drum, it's more fundamental and grounded than that. On a great night, it's a beautiful and inspiring feeling. I look out into the hall and like to think of all the reverberations and vibrations that have soaked into the walls and chairs from all the great bands that have played there over the years.

HEAVY SOUL (1997)

We're words upon a window
Written there in steam
In the heat of the moment
At the birth of a dream
Vapours passing really
So I'm touched by the thought
In the fleeting minutes after
The time that we've come ...

We come and go, you know, where the wind blows
And though I couldn't define
I can only tell you that
I've got a heavy soul

Tuesdays dressed in shearling
Anchored on belief
In the sunlight on the water
Or rain upon a leaf
I'm touched by its beauty
And I hope to touch you too
'cause I still seek the same things
That I once sought to be true

And you know, that's where the wind blows
Tho' I wouldn't be lying, when I tell you that
I got a heavy soul

I was really trying to express my feeling that we are special, that we are touched by nature and beauty and that it's ok to believe that. Water, fire, wind, sun – I always go back to the primal elements. But for the opening couplet I had another romantic image in mind – another suburban image perhaps – of a couple in an old-fashioned steamy café writing love hearts on the window.

SHADOW OF THE SUN (1993)

Do you still feel the same way about it
Like you always said you would
Or has time rewritten everything
Like you never dreamt it could
Remember when we wanted to fly forever
On a magic carpet ride
Well, forever seems a long time
Cutting us down in size
No matter how hard we try

And I could see all I had done
Chasing dreams across the fields
In the shadow of the sun
I plan to have it all while I'm still young
And chase the fields across my dreams
In the shadow of the sun
In the shadow of the sun

Once upon a time I might have told you
But now nothing seems that plain
However much we're changing
There are some things the same
And those same things still say –

I can see all I have done
Just chasing dreams across the fields
In the shadow of the sun
I plan to have it all while I'm still young
And chase the fields across my dreams
In the shadow of the sun
In the shadow of the sun

Funnily enough, I walked past this field again only yesterday and it still does it for me. When I wrote it, I was spending time standing still, looking back, taking stock of what I'd done and wondering where else I could go. For whatever reason, this field became the focus of all that. Again, it brought me back in touch with childhood and that magical thought of what might lie beyond the end of the meadow, or the street or the rainbow.

THE PEBBLE AND THE BOY (2005)

Can you tell the difference between the pebble and the boy
Far away in the distance with the sun in your eyes
Can you see the footprints that have merged with the sand
In your trying to find them, you find only dry land

Can you tell the difference between the pebble and the boy
Can you follow the heartbeats between the boy and the man
If you can, if you can

Can you see the future with every step you take
Yet you feel your no further in your walking away
Can you tell the difference between the pebble and the man
Far away in the ocean, when you're back on dry sand

Can you tell the difference between the pebble and the boy
Can you follow the heartbeats between the boy and the man
If you can, if you can ...

The initial idea came from a Spike Milligan poem in which he meets himself as a boy on a beach and tells his younger self to go back. Being Spike, it's pretty depressing, but I thought the scenario – of being able to meet yourself – was great.